ROUGH DIALECTICS

Sorokin's Philosophy of Value

VIBS

Volume 60

Pitirim A. Sorokin, ca. 1941
(Photo by Fabian Bachrach)

ROUGH DIALECTICS

Sorokin's Philosophy of Value

Palmer Talbutt, Jr.

With contributions by

Lawrence T. Nichols
Pitirim A. Sorokin

Amsterdam - Atlanta, GA 1998

Cover design by Chris Kok based on a photograph, ©1984 by Robert Ginsberg, of statuary by Gustav Vigeland in the Frogner Park, Oslo, Norway.

∞ The paper on which this book is printed meets the requirements of "ISO 9706:1994, Information and documentation - Paper for documents - Requirements for permanence".

ISBN: 90-420-0387-1

Printed in The Netherlands

CONTENTS

FOREWORD

In *Rough Dialectics,* Palmer Talbutt, Jr. characterizes Pitirim A. Sorokin as a philosopher—a public social philosopher of both history and culture. But, after placing Sorokin in the spiritual tradition of Leo Tolstoy, Talbutt goes further and describes Sorokin as a sage, whose "sagecraft" makes room in the house of intellect for religious faith as well as for practical morality.

Focusing on the interplay between urban centers and rural hinterlands, Talbutt portrays Sorokin as a spokesman for devout country folk too often made to look negligible by the "smooth dialectics" of the industrial intelligentsia. In so doing, Talbutt calls much needed attention to Sorokin as a giant of twentieth-century thought, whose universalist message has enduring value in this age of inter- ethnic antagonism and growing disillusionment with civilization itself.

Roger W. Wescott
International Society for the Comparative Study of Civilizations
September 1997

ACKNOWLEDGEMENTS

Many of the chapters in this book began their lives as conference papers or contributions to edited volumes. I am grateful to the attendees of several meetings of the Society for Comparative Studies of Civilization (ISCSC) for their comments on what are now Chapters 13, 14, and 16. In the same spirit, I thank members of the Society for Christian Philosophers and the Society of Asian and Comparative Philosophy for their help with the papers now labeled Chapters 8 and 16, respectively.

Chapters 2, 5, 9, and 14 are modified versions of previously published papers. I thank the editors and publishers of *The Modern Encyclopedia of Russian and Soviety History, Sociologia Internationalis,* and *Sorokin and Civilization* for granting reprint permission. Special thanks go to my friends and colleagues Joseph Ford and Michael Richard, editors of *Sorokin and Civilization,* and organizers of several ISCSC meetings, for their continued intellectual support. Special thanks also go to Lawrence T. Nichols, who contributed two chapters to this work. And last but not least, thanks to Karen Forney of Desktop Techniques, Ed Lamb, and Lisa Huff.

Sergei Sorokin and Bachrach Studios provided the photographs of Pitirim A. Sorokin.

PART ONE

THE BASICS ON SOROKIN

One

INTRODUCTION. ROUGH DIALECTICS: HOW ROUGH IS IT?

Pitirim A. Sorokin offered a masterful view of social and cultural change, in which mounting crises shatter or transform human values. This book examines the distinctiveness of such dialectics; how it is rough, and how rough is it? The shortest answer to the last is "Very rough indeed." This becomes quite apparent through contrast with other accounts, often those with which Americans find the most comfort. Sorokin's thought markedly diverges from, or runs precariously parallel to, such alternatives. Such reinforcements and differentiations can help us catch hold of his extraordinary ideas.

Years ago I was a student in Sorokin's basic course, while simultaneously reading for another Harvard course *The Making of the Modern Mind,* a text written by a Columbia University philosopher, John Herman Randall, Jr. For my first graduate work I went to New York to study at Columbia, taking three semesters with Randall and also doing a research paper on Sorokin for Horace Friess's "Theories of Culture." (That paper served as the distant model for "Sorokin vs. American Thought.") Even today, as I approach all too quickly three-score-and-ten, I judge my two greatest teachers to have been Sorokin and Randall. They scarcely saw eye-to-eye, and perhaps both are watching suspiciously over my shoulders. What to do, what to do, to avoid a countervailing haunting? Let us see how justice might be done, how Sorokin could be grasped more accurately by Americans today, while retaining Randall's rich account of Western thought (especially of the American Golden Age) as a significant foil. I am forced into a dialectical stance in weighing the question. Both great scholars have their own dialectical approaches to history, one rough and the other smoothly progressive.

Despite their respective anti-modernist and modernist stances, Sorokin and Randall share common ground. Sorokin takes the cultural independent variable to be primary, rejecting Marxist sociology of knowledge; his thought has sometimes been characterized as "culturology." Randall, in his turn, takes cultural change as being the main issue for philosophy, and he, unlike some befuddled contemporaries, remained unsnared by Marxism and its narrow economically based mirror-images.

Both scholars see religion as an essential cultural function and neither takes any dogmatic exclusivist religious position. Randall seems to be more secular in tone, but a careful reading of his full work shows him to affirm a sane and sensible religious modernism. Sorokin strongly rejects "tribal altruism-egoisms" productive of strife among ethnic communities. Like Tolstoy, he remains unsnared by communally partisan dogmas and crusading zeal. Indeed, he explicitly denounces the dangers of such movements, of the *hubris* attending the "active ideational" stage, exemplified at times by over-reaching Popes, Czars, Puritans, and Mullahs. Both scholars regard with benignity the world-wide range of faiths, assuming such faiths stay open toward universal altruism. Randall admired Tillich's tolerant breadth of view, as Sorokin had praised Aurobindo and Gandhi. History, history in its entirety, and culture and religion must be taken seriously; fanaticism must be vigorously attacked. So much I took from my two greatest teachers!

One further similarity, though this one carries them in different directions, is their lack of sympathy for Kant. In a broad sense, both scholars want to show culture as mediating reality. Randall prefers the ontological, anti-dualist emphasis to the epistemological, along with his father who was a religious modernist, rejecting theological liberalisms like Albrecht Ritschl's as "mere compromises." "*Raus mit Kant!*" declares the younger Randall, for whom a better alternative is monistic idealism, flowing easily into a realistic naturalism. Yet one finds ghostly traces of Kant in Randall's acknowledgments of diverse functions of culture, for example, science and religion. As these are presented, his tone differs from that of his teacher John Dewey.

Sorokin has a poor ear for Western European philosophy in general, and he looks upon Kant as an agnostic paving the way for still more unfortunate skepticisms. Sorokin wants to affirm the value of intuition construed in terms of a Superconscious. Randall is far more this-worldly as to the sources of knowledge, even while he concedes that "mythic" religious expressions have some value, as does Platonic or Platonistic "Wisdom."

Sorokin is the subject of this volume. Randall, perhaps the most distinguished American historian of Western philosophy, has served for me personally as a touchstone for Sorokin's startling departures from Western conventional wisdom on philosophy. Randall exemplifies a subtle and most convincing version of progressive dialectic, and this is a helpful foil against Sorokin's rough variety. Randall saw great philosophies as developed from the impacts of major scientific traditions or advances upon older institutional values. This remained a central theme in the Columbia approach to the history of philosophy.

Sorokin, by contrast, pursued a cultural dialectic far rougher than Hegel's waltz-time, even than the Marxist class-warfare so hopefully destined to smooth out into a classless idyll. It was also rough in its untidiness, lacking philosophical or ideological neatness, which derives in part from its inclusiveness and vague boundaries. This dialectic works on all sorts of levels, where rough, often calamitous, intrusions erode and transform the values objectified in sociocultural reality. Sorokin wrote extensively upon famine, war, and revolution, and upon those events rightly denominated "circumstances beyond our control." This pushed him up into the longest views of historical sociology and the broadest kind of macrosociology. All was destined to put him at loggerheads with urban microsociologists, with their managerial optimism so smugly ensconced in a happier world than that of Sorokin's youth and early maturity. The roughness of Sorokin's revolutionary, then counter-revolutionary, polemical style carried over into his academic life. He rode roughshod over opponents and the conceptual distinctions usually favored by moderns. His was not so such an effete "post-modernism" as a vigorous anti-modernism.

What I find to serve best as a master key for understanding Sorokin is the notion of "rough dialectic," wherein the greatest share of the conflicts can be seen as polarized by the radial contrariety between power centers and their inner and outer peripheries, hinterlands and outlands. Other conflicts and adversities no doubt enter in, but the radial contrast stands out. Social and economic class differences have been metaphorically set on vertical vectors. Their opposite poles reflect values and persons' self-images as to what they are, and are not. Where physical distance enters in with a radius of distance between, say, the city mouse and the country mouse, complex repertoires begin to elaborate the picture. The radial contrariety serves as warp to the vertical woofs, especially in extensive civilizations such as the Russian and American. Individuals may strongly identify with one sort of pole or another. Sorokin's roots were deep, and he affirmed their value vigorously. The die had been cast with Sorokin's own regional background in northern Russia among the Komi people and his work with the peasant Social Revolutionaries. Americans are aware of their own radial contrariety and it has been affirmed by Emerson, Jefferson, and the populists, but with nothing like the fierce antagonism of Sorokin. Why?

The First World War and its attendant miseries had also heavily impacted on Spengler and Toynbee. Truly, Spengler, Toynbee, and Sorokin constitute the twentieth-century triumvirate of speculative philosophers of history. Theirs were all "social philosophies in an age of crisis," but Sorokin had by far the most drastic personal experiences. The wheel of fortune had carried him higher, professionally and politically, and cast him down lower. Both Westernizing and Slavophil influences were strong in Sorokin's thought; the jolts given to Sorokin by Bolshevik victories over the Kerensky administration, the Constituent Assembly, and his own group of right wing Social Revolutionaries participating in a northern Russian campaign, successively undermined his Westernizing liberalism. Late 1917 through 1922 was an extraordinarily harsh time for the Sorokins.

Sorokin had reached the height of his political status when he entered the Provisional Government as Kerensky's secretary. But he had to watch in frustration lost opportunities to thwart Lenin and to propitiate Kornilov. (Some of those opinions of his may have been partly shaped in hindsight.) Sorokin's low points would come with the Bolshevik coup, with the closing of the Constituent Assembly, his first arrest subsequently, and then, as the very nadir, the collapse of the counterrevolutionary efforts to which he committed himself in the late summer and fall of 1918. Seen in retrospect, that counterrevolutionary activity associated with the Allied occupation of Archangel was foredoomed.

The German victories, Lenin's promises of "Peace, Land, and Bread," even Trotsky's temporizing expedient of "Neither war nor peace," had had the effect of peeling away peasant support from rightist Social Revolutionaries (SR). And most trained officers had been alienated by revolutionary trends within the Russian army. The Archangel revolt-plus-intervention was out of step with virtually all strategic considerations (Halliday 1958, pp. 23ff., 37ff). Consider the timing and purposes of the Czech Legion's Trans-Siberian movements after the fall of the Provisional Government; the limited aims and cross-purposes of the intervening Allied expeditions; the feeble enthusiasm of only the more prosperous Archangel citizenry; and the narrow political base of the Allies' chosen Russian agent, Chaikovsky; his appointments were limited to tactless choices of rightist Social Revolutionaries. (The British General Poole and his aides had been infuriated at this.) Adding to the danger, the Allied troops had no convenient way of distinguishing Bolshevik from anti-Bolshevik peasants. Sorokin had the near hopeless task of recruiting and organizing peasants to fight the Bolsheviks. Soon he was on the run and eventually turned himself in to his enemies to reduce reprisals against surviving sympathizers. Sorokin, rightly or wrongly, came to feel betrayed by the Western Allies, and to regard SR resistance as totally futile.

This experience gave a shattering jolt to Sorokin, shifting his center of gravity from Westernizing optimism to a more Slavophil "mystical anarchism." (That position had a strong Tolstoyan color, as did Sorokin's abjuration of direct political action in favor of a return to scholarship, whereupon Lenin was persuaded by some Bolshevik colleagues to pardon Sorokin and to write "Some Valuable Admissions by Pitirim A. Sorokin" for *Pravda.*)

Yet there were strong mental reservations associated with Sorokin's withdrawal from active politics. His revolutionary and counter-revolutionary energies and his intense polemical skills were now channeled exclusively in scholarly directions, though often so as to be made available for a wide literate public. He was, and remained, a distruster of establishments, whether Czarist, Bolshevik, or liberal Western, and also of academic orthodoxies. He was again unwelcome for his speaking and writing, especially for *The Factor of Hunger in Human Affairs,* and was very lucky to have been given exile rather than execution in 1922, for which an official was severely rebuked. The tenor of Sorokin's later career had been forged. Milder, decorous, and more conventional colleagues and rivals would again and again be taken aback or infuriated by Sorokin, whose rootages and commitments were so different from their more placid backgrounds.

The "radial contrariety" in perspectives and values as between hinterlanders and those identifying with urban power centers will come in for detailed discussion later. Suffice it to note here that Sorokin turned decisively away from confidence in modernism and progress back to his own regional roots. This meant that managerial political science and economics were minimized in favor of a long view of history and of cultural change. Cultural and social changes were to be seen as powered by crises; Sorokin's major works and his critiques of modern social theories reflect this. One point made in his rural-urban sociology was his doubt about the value of "over-urbanization" and this recurred in later attacks on "overripe sensate" culture. He took an adversarial stance from the hinterland against the power center.

The roughness of the personal political shock to Sorokin fed the roughness of his anti-modernist dialectic. While Sorokin largely sympathized with the views of Toynbee and Spengler, he still criticized their limitations. His own searing insights had been too dearly bought for him to be restrained by academic politesse, even for his highly regarded prophetic peers. Microsociologists and progressives could expect no mercy at all. Toynbee looked upon Sorokin with friendly and rueful good humor; both had enjoyed good exchanges at the Salzburg meeting of the International Society for the Comparative Study of Civilizations.

The following essays show the drama and the rough dialectic of controversy which it opened in Academe far from Russia. Sorokin's "Tolstoy as Philosopher" was written in 1914, well before the first Russian Revolution. Nichols's essay needs no supplement in its affirming of Tolstoy's influence. Three brief points should still be made. (1) The content of idealistic and ideational cultures, as presented in the *Dynamics,* is highly reminiscent of Tolstoy's philosophy, as Sorokin construes it; likewise that is true of much that Sorokin had to say on altruism and its conditions.

(2) Tolstoy's work exemplifies the radial contrast between urban and regional values most strongly, as does his life. *War and Peace* sets Napoleon as a shallow urban type against the more intuitive and deeply Russian Kutuzov. History is erroneously thought to be mastered by Napoleon, while it is more like a storm to be ridden out for Kutuzov. The honest Rostovs on their estate are more authentically human than the Frenchified aristocrats of St. Petersburg. And Natasha is nearly undone by a scheming city slicker (much as is Squire Wardle's sister by Jingle in the more comic *Pickwick Papers.).* Art and its values are construed regionally and religiously by Tolstoy in *What Is Art?* And Sorokin drew upon this book to characterize ideational and sensate types in art.

(3) The gist of Sorokin's paper, a spirited defense of calling Tolstoy a philosopher, raises a self-referential question. Is Sorokin himself a philosopher, and if so, in what sense? Surely if Tolstoy is one, so is Sorokin. Both seriously pursue wisdom, though Tolstoy is more a sage-artist while Sorokin is a sage-scholar. In the broad sense that "philosophy is for everyone," then Sorokin assuredly and consciously philosophizes. Distinctions can be drawn respecting the audiences addressed. Let us say that Tolstoy, as a popular writer and sage, and Sorokin, as a former journalist and later a scholar producing works for an extended readership, were at least "popular philosophers." The sage's appeal is to folk-wisdom and widely shared values,

often religious in nature. Such work is frequently regional in tone.

On the whole, "public philosophy" (so called by Walter Lippmann and others) addresses citizens on a more sophisticated level; this makes more demands for its appreciation, while its civic and justificatory function is more at home in an urban, often academic, context. Sorokin offers more "public philosophy" in the range of his weightier books. The philosopher here speaks to various professionals.

"Public philosophy" thus lies midway between "popular philosophy" and "professional philosophy" which restricts its audience not to different sorts of professionals but to other philosophers. Professional philosophy has sharp limitations. Sorokin was no such philosopher. Indeed, he defied many of the most beloved premises of modern Western philosophers, let alone those of the professionals. (Much of America's Golden Age philosophy, with Dewey, James, Royce, and Santayana, had been "public" rather than "professional" in its accessibility.)

What about the philosophical fields into which Sorokin moved? We can say social philosophy, speculative philosophy of history, philosophy of culture, and philosophy of value. Philosophy of value probably holds up best as the center of gravity for Sorokin's work, with one proviso. He sees values in their concrete social and historical expressions, as they superimpose upon material vehicles and are internalized in conscious agents. Axiologists and philosophical analysts alike engage in far more abstract examinations. F.R. Cowell is right in emphasizing the social concreteness of Sorokin's approach to value. Philosophy of culture would be another option for taking a view of Sorokin, but value for Sorokin neatly co-implicates both the social and the cultural. Westerners might associate "culture" with ivory-tower aestheticism, or with Matthew Arnold's "sweetness and light." Sorokin's is a rougher account than such suggestions would allow.

Was Sorokin a philosopher or was he not? To recapitulate, he was at least as much of a sage as Leo Tolstoy or even as Lao-tse, with whose attacks on bureaucrats he sympathized. Furthermore, one may selectively draw from his works, given some reconstructive effort, a philosophy of culture and a philosophy of value. And he has as much of a speculative philosophy of history as do Spengler and Toynbee.

So far so good. The phrase "public philosopher" applies well to Sorokin since he, like Augustine, Aquinas, Comte, Marx, and Toynbee, addressed a broad, educated audience. A line might be drawn among public philosophers, between those like Plato and Aristotle who are mainly "philosophers' philosophers," and those who grind non-philosophical axes, who use philosophy for other purposes, though these are often intellectually respectable. Augustine and Aquinas made philosophy subservient to theology; Marx to political ideology. Although Comte was taken as a "typical French philosopher" by Sorokin, basically he ground two non-philosophical axes. First, by justifying the possibility of positivist social science, and secondly, by discrediting theological and metaphysical traditions.

In Sorokin's own case, he used philosophical distinctions and arguments in the service of two aims. He sought to establish a sociocultural science, in which cultural meanings can be shown to cohere with social movements and to relate to the historical occasions that force their changes. Secondly, unlike Comte, he aimed at rehabilitating pre-modern traditions as meaningful and as recurrent, though in modified and improved forms. (Sorokin did not so much repudiate Comtean social science as amplify it.)

Let me pose an implicit problem which the chapters in this book will be circling about. How is Sorokin to be made available to Americans whose allegiance is to some version of progressive dialectic? I have already indicated that the John Herman Randalls, both senior and junior, hold a highly plausible version of this liberal view. Sorokin's dialectic is a rough one, particularly conditioned by his sufferings and those of Russia. How are two such dialectics, neither of which is naive, to be accommodated to one another? The book's conclusion will return to this issue.

Something should be said about this book's order. The short introduction broaches the tough question of how Sorokin's rough dialectic can be accommodated to American progressivist thought, and the discussion will largely turn about that issue. Part One presents basic facts about Sorokin, including a paper by Sorokin himself showing the early Tolstoy influence and one by Larry Nichols reaffirming that point. Part Two features a number of my Neo-Sorokinian chapters on philosophical and religious systems, in terms of typological statics and dialectical dynamics. These metaphilosophical and metacultural discussions connect up with Sorokin's sociocultural dynamics, presented here in interrelated sequence. Part Three leads up to, and follows from, the intended centerpiece of my interpretation, "Dialectic Against Modernity." The Conclusion, entitled "The Rough and the Smooth," draws upon comparisons with two progressivist liberals, John Herman Randall, Jr., and Talcott Parsons, to make broader points about "rough dialectics" in general.

Two

SOROKIN'S LIFE AND CAREER

This short biographical sketch was written during my sabbatical leave for The Modern Encyclopedia of Russian and Soviet History. *I am obliged to the publishers, Academic International Press, for permission to abridge it here. Research was done at Harvard University, and I was especially appreciative for an interiew with Robert Bales. It enabled me to reach a much better understanding of the relations between Parsons and Sorokin, which are treated at greater length later in this book.*

The reference to the original is as follows: Palmer Talbutt, "Sorokin, Pitirim Aleksandrovich" in *The Modern Encyclopedia of Russian and Soviet History* (Gulf Breeze, Fl.: Academic International Press, 1976-1994), Vol. 36: pp. 177-81.

Pitirim A. Sorokin was born in the village of Turia in the Yarenskii District of Vologda Province on 21 January 1889. His father, Aleksander Prokopevich, was an itinerant artisan of Russian birth, while his mother was of the Komi people, belonging to the Ugro-Finnish group; they were bi-lingual and fairly well-to-do peasants who had never known serfdom. After his mother died three years later, young Pitirim and his eldest brother shared their father's life for seven years, then broke up a year before their father's death, while supporting themselves by carrying on his itinerant trade of painting icons. Later, Sorokin won a tiny scholarship in a nearby village grade school from which he graduated in 1903 and was commended for another scholarship at Khrenovo Teachers' Seminary, Kostroma Province.

While there, and once caught up in revolutionary fervor, Sorokin became a leader of the non-Marxist Socialist Revolutionary party and was arrested in late 1906 for his subversion. After four months in prison, he briefly wandered as an agitator before traveling to St. Petersburg in 1907. There, he fed himself as best he could while attending night school and enjoying forbidden political activities. Staying at Velikii Ustiug, Volgoda Province, with an aunt and uncle in 1909, he won high marks in the examination of maturity for university admission. Once back in St. Petersburg, he enrolled at the Psycho-Neurological Institute, partly because sociology was taught there, and not at the University. A year later, shifting to the University of St. Petersburg and once granted yet another scholarship, he signed on with the department of law and economics. During his junior year he published his first full-scale scholarly volume, on penology, and in 1914, he graduated not only with a first-class diploma but with the lofty status of one permitted to stay to prepare for a professorship. In 1915, he became a Magistrant of Criminal Law. Law, penology, and sociology were his fields of research, but he continued his political work. Tsarist authorities had jailed him briefly twice before. Nonetheless, Sorokin remained loyal to that moderate wing of the Socialist Revolutionaries which fought against any separate peace with the Germans. Throughout the turmoil of the first revolution, he was in the very thick of things within the local unit of his party, pushing through an early resolution supporting the Provisional Government, quarreling with leftist editorial colleagues on the paper *Delo Naroda* (People's Cause), and resigning in late April to co-found *Volya Naroda* (The Will of the People) and to help set up an All-Russian Peasant's conference for May—from which a Peasants' Soviet emerged with Sorokin as a member of the Executive Committee. On one significant day, 26 May 1917, he married Elena Petrovna Baratynskaia and also enjoyed a cordial visit from the Czech leader, Professor Thomas Masaryk.

In July, amidst deteriorating conditions within and without the bitterly contending Soviets, Sorokin was offered any of three positions in the Provisional Government, from which he chose the secretaryship to Kerensky. Yet Sorokin saw that government as hopelessly weak and as fatally doomed to Bolshevism by the Kornilov-Kerensky clash of late August.

After the debacle of the October Revolution, Sorokin's own plight became perilous. Only luck and, at drastic junctures, the friendly memories of old revolutionary allies saved his skin. His election as a deputy to the Constitutional Assembly meant little as protection, the outvoted Bolsheviks being determined to prevent its meeting. On 2 January 1918, he was imprisoned in the Fortress of Peter and Paul, but was released 57 days later through the efforts of one Kramaroff. Returning first to "cat-and-mouse" revolutionary journalism in Moscow and then to an anti-Bolshevik mission to Velikii Ustiug, Vologda, and Archangel, he was disillusioned at the delays and broken promises of the British expeditionary force, given their failure to chase the fleeing Communists. Sorokin hid for two months, then decided to turn himself in to the Communist authorities at Velikii Ustiug to protect his family and others. Under sentence of death among other victims, Sorokin waited six weeks expecting to be shot. Lenin himself, at the urging of fellow Bolsheviks Piatakov and Karakhan, reversed that decision in a bid for the support of scientists, non-Bolshevik revolutionaries, and those who admired them. Lenin wrote an article for *Pravda* on 21 November, "Valuable Admissions by Pitirim A. Sorokin," which Sorokin was shown on 13 December before being freed three days later.

Back at the University of Petrograd, where Sorokin returned to his professorship of Sociology, living and political conditions were bad and bound to worsen. With the follies of Bolshevik policy, wholesale starvation occurred in 1920-1921. Sorokin did not undertake a third volume to his *System of Sociology*, published in the spring of 1920, but rather turned to the study of hunger. Forbidden to teach in the fall of 1921, he looked at the horrible effects of famine in his nation. *The Influence of Hunger on Human Behavior* appeared heavily censored in May 1922. (Only in 1975 did this book appear in the West, translated by Mrs. Sorokin.) In the summer of 1922, many noted scholars were jailed; this time, as it turned out, they were to be banished instead of being executed. Sorokin, in hiding, turned himself in to the Moscow Chekha, this being far safer than their office in St. Petersberg. Next, he obtained his passport from Karakhan himself at the Commissariat of Foreign Affairs. The Sorokins left for Berlin on 23 September 1922. Later, they learned that the officials who had let them depart had been rebuked and that all remaining printings of his work on famine were destroyed.

Once in Berlin, Sorokin was soon invited by Thomas Masaryk, now President of Czechoslovakia, to come to Prague. While in exile, Sorokin began a number of scholarly projects, such as studies in rural sociology and his *Sociology of Revolution*, later translated into English and published in 1925. Sorokin was invited to lecture in the United States in early 1924. He left Europe in October 1923 for a new career, already persuaded of the inadequacies of positivistic progressivism.

Once in New York, Sorokin studied English, received speaking engagements, and energetically arranged some publications. After a stay at Vassar and lectures at the Universities of Illinois and Wisconsin, Sorokin was commended by E.A. Ross to the University of Minnesota. There he was hired as a visiting professor, first for the summer of 1924, then for the next year. Mrs. Sorokin came to join her husband in March 1924. Sorokin remained at Minnesota until 1930; Mrs. Sorokin completed her doctorate there and taught at Hamline University.

Scholarly volumes such as *The Sociology of Revolution, Social Mobility, Contemporary Theories of Sociology,* and, in association with Carle Zimmerman, *Principles of Rural-Urban Sociology,* and with Zimmerman and C.J. Galpin, *A Systematic Source-Book in Rural Sociology* (1925, 1927, 1928, 1930), along with numerous articles, well fixed Sorokin's reputation. In the spring of 1929 he was invited to give guest lectures at Harvard and, in the fall, was offered an appointment as Harvard's first professor of sociology for the academic year 1930-1931. By mutual agreement, that position was to be the nucleus of a new department absorbing some of the faculty from economics and also the small department of social ethics. Sorokin chaired the interdisciplinary committee that made the plans, opening Harvard's new program in the fall of 1931. The Sorokins' two sons were born in 1931 and 1932.

Organizational work, instruction of graduate students, and the maturation of a major research project, already conceived before his going to Cambridge, Massachusetts, absorbed so much of Sorokin's time that his astounding rate of producing books apparently slowed. This appearance was deceptive, however, since in 1937 the first three volumes of his magnum opus, *Social and Cultural Dynamics*, were published. The fourth volume, drawing conclusions and summarizing, appeared four years later. For this work, research associates in Cambridge and also in Prague had been needed to examine and classify vast amounts of material.

Sorokin's "integralist" historical sociology and theory of fluctuations between "ideational" (religious), "idealistic" (a mediating or harmonizing type), and "sensate" (empiricist) cultures was rooted in his Russian background and his revulsion against optimistic and liberal progressivism. His own change of heart dated at least from the early 1920s, and various factors, such as his expressed doubts about psychological, biological, and environmental theories of sociology, betokened yet stronger attacks upon naturalism. To some extent during his Minnesota years, and decidedly later, professional American sociologists, particularly through reviews in establishment journals, expressed reservations about Sorokin. With the publication of the *Dynamics*, which was widely reviewed with both praise and condemnation, Sorokin had put his cards on the table. His many later works, while often fresh contributions, were bound to allude to or imply methodological notions underlying that magisterial and highly controversial work. Indeed, his important activity heading the Harvard Center in Creative Altruism in the late 1940s not only reflected the early Tolstoyan influence upon his life, but stood as a practical corollary to Sorokin's diagnosis of the crisis of "overripe sensate" civilization. In his reformist and prophetic zeal, Sorokin employed his considerable polemical and rhetorical skills.

Even with his popularity among the American public, shown by attendance at his Lowell lectures in 1941, and wide recognition abroad, the professional world took Sorokin less than seriously. At the time of his resignation as chairman (1942), another Harvard colleague, Talcott Parsons, whose structural-functionalist views were felt to be more relevant by American professionals, was assuming greater leadership. The contrast between Sorokin's "integralist" historical sociology (sometimes misleadingly called "culturology") and the temporally short-range but broadly conceived approach of Parsons is sharp, as were Sorokin's objections. The disadvantage of being a "lone wolf" is the chance of being outnumbered; the Department of Sociology expanded into a Department of Social Relations and did not reconstitute itself until 1970.

Yet Sorokin kept busy, while less in his departmental mainstream, producing *Society, Culture, and Personality* (1947), a work from which any serious student of social studies or humanities will profit, and after this his important researches upon altruism, until reaching the age of 70. That Sorokin is not only a "Culturologist," though he stresses culture and values, may also be seen in respects, noticed by Sorokin himself: he commented on the ways in which his work anticipates various basic details in Parsons's 1951 book on the social system.

In the still-creative years after Sorokin's retirement and preceding his death in 1968, more international honors came to him, as did belatedly (by write-in ballot) the presidency of the American Sociological Association. Such recognitions, and the republishing of certain key books were seen as appropriate and overdue by admiring scholars, such as his old colleagues Carle Zimmerman, Arnold Toynbee, and also F.R. Cowell. In his day, Sorokin strode upon a much wider stage than any afforded by politics, ordinary or academic. His transcending of politics allowed him to attend to sociocultural systems of greater extent and duration than political systems, whose crises can then be seen in a far larger context.

As sources for learning about Sorokin, his own autobiographical writings are indispensable. But aside from those, an excellent new study, by Barry V. Johnston (1995) has just come out. Johnston's book gives a full, well-researched account of Sorokin's impact and the scholarly reactions to his work.

Three

L. N. TOLSTOY AS A PHILOSOPHER

PITIRIM A. SOROKIN

Lawrence T. Nichols has translated this most significant paper written by Sorokin at age 25. It throws light on Sorokin's "mystical anarchism" and his lifelong non-conformism. I am most appreciative for Nichols's permission to use the article here. It anticipates much in Sorokin's discussion of the superconscious, altruism, and creativity.

This paper has been stylistically re-edited, to conform as far as possible with current standards. There is some resistance to carrying this out, given the references: Tolstoy's "Way of Life" was published either in 1881 or 1887, for example. So the scholarly apparatus must be taken with a grain of salt; that would have been true in any case, in view of the early date of the Russian version.

1.

That L. N. Tolstoy is a great artist no one will dispute; but that Tolstoy is a great thinker and, specifically, a philosopher, remains a matter of doubt. Evidence of the existence of such doubt is provided by Prof. A. A. Isayev's book, *Count L. N. Tolstoy as a Thinker*, and this certainly is not an isolated example, since there is a series of other articles which treat Tolstoy as a thinker in a similarly skeptical manner. "One experiences disillusionment," says Prof. Isayev, "when one attentively follows the philosophy and publicism of Tolstoy. First and foremost, the eye is struck by numerous contradictions. These concern not only details, but fundamental positions as well" (p. 228). "The numerous contradictions can be explained only by the fact that Tolstoy in his works often adheres to the methods of a journalist. No doubt he glanced through and looked over a large number of books. But it is not apparent that he attentively studied and considered from all sides the questions upon which he hastens to express his opinion" (p. 229).

"The reader gets an unpleasant impression from Tolstoy's urge to be eccentric, his irrepressible inclination for paradox," and so on (p. 230). From the foregoing citations it is clear that Prof. Isayev's verdict is rather severe. One is forced to this conclusion, because the author makes use of a whole array of evidence in indicting Tolstoy: figures, facts, observations, and so forth. However, in spite of this, we consider his verdict to be inaccurate, and advance the opposite thesis, contending that in reality Tolstoy is a great philosopher.

2.

In our opinion, the negative attitude toward the philosophy of Tolstoy is based, in significant degree, upon a misunderstanding, namely, that the requirements placed before Tolstoy are not the requirements which ought to be placed before a philosopher. For this reason, it becomes necessary to say a few words about what philosophy is, and what its problems of study are.

It is well known that, up to now, philosophy has been seeking a definition of itself. At one time it was the *alma mater* of all the sciences, but in the course of cultural development the sciences have little by little distinguished themselves from philosophy. Until recent times, an eclectic summa was understood as belonging to philosophy: logic, epistemology, ethics, aesthetics—but now even these sciences are little by little differentiating themselves from philosophy and are becoming independent of it.

It becomes necessary to seek a new *definitio artis philosophandi* (a definition of philosophy). Some define it as the generalization and systematization of the facts given by the particular sciences (Spencer), others as "the science concerned with principles" (Uberweg), and still others as the science of thought and values (Rickert and Windelband), and so on (Rickert 1910).

Without entering into any substantial criticism of all these definitions (which would lead us astray), let us note that they are all either without a grounding in logic, or else present only words instead of conceptions (the school of value), or else do not accord with the essence of the matter. But, along with this, they contain some kernel of truth—insofar as they consider philosophy as embracing the world in its entirety.

It has already been some time since a definition of philosophy was proposed by E. V. DeRoberty, which has been reiterated in his most recent works, and particularly in his article, *"Le problème sociologique et le problème philosophique"* (1911). "Philosophical thought is profoundly different from scientific thought," writes DeRoberty. "The philosopher (the metaphysician as well as the theologian) utilizes the most mature ideas of his environment and his times (or the "particular syntheses" of the different sciences), in order with their help to erect a new edifice: *a general synthesis of the world*." Science is always analytic and hypothetical; philosophy always synthetic and apodictic. The criteria of scientific "truth" and of philosophic "truth" are entirely distinct, as are the criteria of "truth" in the sciences and in works of art. Just as aesthetic phenomena, along with science, constitute a distinct species of social thought, so philosophy, along with these species, constitutes a self-sufficient *modus* of social thought. Similar to this understanding is the definition of Prof. Petrazhitsky, of philosophy as "the theory *of the real in general*" (Petrazhitsky 1908).

G. Simmel in his latest work approaches the very same definition of philosophy. The most characteristic feature of philosophy, he says, is the desire "to think without premises" (Simmel 1911, p. 8). From this feature of philosophy, it follows that neither the methods nor the truths of the particular sciences are mandatory for it. Since all the sciences begin with premises, and since no premises are mandatory for philosophy, philosophy has the right to consider any proposition dictated to it by its system. This explains why various philosophies proceed from various premises. *"Das Recht und die Pflicht der Philosophie, sich mit grosserer Unabhängigkeit von dem Gegebenen, als sie in andern Erkenntnisprovinzen bestehet, ihr Objekt selbst zu fixieren, bringen es mit sich, dass die verschiedenen philosophischen Lehren auch von grundsätzlich vershiedenen Problemstellungen aüsgehen*" (Simmel 1911, p. 10).

Whatever their differences in composition, all philosophical systems have something in common, namely, *a comprehension of the world in its entirety and unity. "Mann kann den Philosophen vielleicht als denjenigen bezeichnen, der das aufnehmende und reagierende Organ für die Ganzheit des Seins hat,*" says Simmel (can one then grant the title of philosopher to anyone having a faculty for apprehending and responding to *being in its entirety*?). Every person is always striving for one thing or another: for the guarantee of bread, for the teaching of the church, and so forth; while the philosopher (whatever he may be studying)—as philosopher—always desires to grasp the entirety of the world, to construct a synthesis. For this reason he "has a special sense for perceiving the *integrity* of things and of life, and for the possibility of translating this inner contemplation, or this feeling, of integrity into concepts and their combinations" (Simmel 1911, p. 12). The history of philosophy gives complete support to this definition. Every philosopher, as philosopher, strives for just this comprehension of the unity and entirety of things. They have seen this unity now in matter (Democritus), now in ideas (Plato), now in the spirit (Hegel), now in the will (Schopenhauer), and so forth.

This comprehension of the entirety of the world, of its unity in diversity, is possible in two ways: either, *proceeding from an indivisible external absolute, we bring the whole world to the absolute, and lead it into the soul; or else, proceeding from the depths of our "I," we construct the whole world out of it.* The first way is the way of mysticism; the second way is the way of solipsism and Kantianism. ("The whole world is my representation of it," or "The whole world is the content of my consciousness.")

From these characteristics of philosophy it follows that the criteria of value and "truth" for philosophy and science are not one and the same. Science always begins with premises, and, during the study of a phenomenon, analyzes it. Its syntheses are always partial syntheses. Philosophy, on the other hand, desires to "think without premises." It is essentially a synthesis of the world, and, as such, has its own criterion of "truth," distinct from that of science, just as aesthetic phenomena have their own criterion of "truth" which does not resemble scientific truth.

The "truth" of philosophy, in Simmel's opinion, is the *typicality* of the reaction *of the human spirit to the unity and entirety of the world*, or—to put it another way—*philosophy is a temperament considered through a picture of the world* (Simmel 1911, pp. 23-24). Philosophy, says Simmel, "*Zeichnet nicht die Objektivität der Dinge nach—das tun die 'Wissenschaften' ins engeren Sinne,—sondern die Typen menschlichen Geistigkeit, wie sie sich je an einer bestimmten Auffassung der Dinge offenbaren.*" Therefore it is entirely possible that "*ist Wahrheit überhaupt nicht der ganz angemessene Begriff, um den Wert einer Philosophie auszudrucken*" (Simmel 1911, pp. 27-30). The teachings of Schelling, Schopenhauer, Plato, and others have long since been refuted from the scientific point of view, because they "contradict the facts." They, however, possess their own value and truth, on whose account they are as necessary as the sciences (Bergson 1910, 1912).

From what has been said, it becomes completely clear why

philosophy has always studied certain problems: "the essence of things," the "I" and the reciprocal relations between the "I" and the "not I," the meaning and value of the world and of its development, and the meaning of our life. . . . These four problems constitute the substratum of every philosophy, and follow immediately from the definition of philosophy given above.

Having with these few strokes defined the characteristics of philosophy and of the philosopher (the strokes are a digression, but in view of the unclear conception of "philosophy," they are indispensable for what follows), let us return to our theme.

3.

"All who turn to the science of our day not for the purpose of satisfying idle curiosity, nor in order to play a role in science, nor to make a living at science, but simply in order to answer direct, simple, vital questions find that science answers for them thousands of complex and learned questions—but not that one question to which every intelligent person seeks an answer: 'What am I, and how am I to live?'" So writes L. N. Tolstoy in *The False Sciences.* In saying this, Tolstoy immediately advances two of the fundamental problems of philosophy, and marks out the border between science and philosophy. That this distinction between science and philosophy, or "knowledge and wisdom" (understanding), is not accidental, is evident from the whole character of the world view of Lev Nikolayevich.

"The wise are not always the learned, and the learned are not always the wise," he says, citing Lao-Tsu (*The False Sciences*, p. 15). "Experimental sciences, when pursued for their own sake and cultivated without any *guiding philosophical idea*, are like a face without eyes," he says farther on (p. 11). In the same work, in Section 7, he distinguishes two types of ignorance: "natural ignorance," and the "ignorance" of "the truly wise," by which he understands a mass of knowledge not essential to life, not answering the basic questions of what am I, and how am I to live.

I will not extend these citations further. From what has been said, it is already evident that Tolstoy clearly and sharply distinguishes two species of science: the true and the false sciences. For the moment, this is quite sufficient. (Whether or not Tolstoy contradicts this, we shall see farther on.) And thus Tolstoy distinguishes false knowledge and true wisdom or philosophy. . . . This gives us the right, and provides the basis for studying Tolstoy as a philosopher.

Above we noted that the fundamental problems of philosophy, following from its essence as a world-embracing system, appeared to be: (1) the problem of the essence of the world; (2) of the "I"; (3) of the relationship or knowledge of the "I" and "not I"; and (4) of the value and meaning of being . . . . These problems always constitute the essence of every philosophy, and every philosophy, once it has assumed something for its basic premise, answers all these questions in a deductive manner in agreement with its premise. In this agreement with its foundation is contained also the criterion of its "truth," of its typical response to the unity of the world.

Did Tolstoy occupy himself with these questions? The answer is clear: the entire activity of Tolstoy the non-artist consists in nothing other than the resolution of these questions, a resolution not by means of scientific analysis but by means of a philosophic, world-embracing synthesis. . . . Having assumed a definite premise, Tolstoy constructs upon it in a consistent manner an entire system of philosophy in which each part follows with a logical inevitability from the preceding premises and appears as an indispensable link in this well proportioned edifice of philosophic creativity. In its turn, the edifice conditions the smallest details of the world view and conduct of Lev Nikolayevich. Therefore, to remove isolated parts of this system, as Prof. Isayev does, and then to criticize them from the point of view of "the facts" and the particular sciences is to not understand the essence of philosophy. Tolstoy, like Hegel, could reply to such criticism: "then so much the worse for the facts."

It is true that Tolstoy does not employ sophisticated philosophical terminology: "the transcendent, the immanent, the phenomenal, the noumenal," etc., whose presence often relates a man to "philosophers." But it is hardly necessary to point out that the essence of the matter is not altered by whether one employs sophisticated words in the resolution of problems, or whether one speaks in simple, comprehensible words. (Why Tolstoy is "simple," moreover, has reasons of its own. See below.)

4.

What is Tolstoy's response to the fundamental question of philosophy: "What is the essence of the world (things *an und für sich*)? Where lies its oneness in the appearance of diverse, multifaceted forms?" Above, we noted two types of world-embracing philosophic syntheses: the way proceeding from the absolute found outside the "I," and the way proceeding from our "I." Tolstoy unquestionably takes the first path. Let us try to briefly outline his response.

"I know that there is within me *that without which nothing would exist. And that thing is what I call God*." So responds Tolstoy to the first question of philosophy. "Every man who thinks about what he is cannot help but see that he is not everything, but is a particular, separate part of *something*," he continues. "And having realized this, a man ordinarily thinks that this *something* from which he is separated is the material world which he sees. . . . But as soon as a man thinks about this a bit more deeply, or learns what the wise have thought about the matter, he realizes that his *something* from which people feel themselves separated is not the *material world*, but something else. If a man thinks about it more deeply he will realize that the material world which never ends and which has no limit *is not something genuine, but only our fantasy* (last part my italics), and that for this reason that *something* from which we feel ourselves separated is something having no beginning and no end, neither in time nor in space, and is something immaterial, spiritual, which man acknowledges as his source of life, and is that which the wise have called and call God" (Tolstoy [1881] 1887, "God," pp.2-3).

And so the condition of every being, the basis of the entire world, is God. *God is that logically prior being without whom nothing is comprehensible and nothing is possible.* "Prove that God exists!" exclaims Tolstoy. "Could there be a more foolish notion than to prove God? To prove the existence of God is the same as providing the existence of one's own life. Prove it to whom? How? Why? *If there is not God, then there is nothing*. How can He be proven? God is. It is unnecessary for us to prove His existence" (p. 16; cf. section 5, p. 15).

Since the essence of things, the foundation of being, is God, and the physical world is only something which seems to be, "our fantasy," one might ask what are the characteristics of God. What is He with respect to ourselves, and what is He Himself *an und für sich,* and do we apprehend Him or not? If we apprehend, then how and why is such apprehension of Him possible?

Analyzing Tolstoy's understanding of God, we meet first of all a whole series of negative definitions.

First of all, *God is something immaterial and spiritual.* Since God is the basis of every being and life, and the corporeal is only something which seems to be, it follows that God cannot be physical.

The second characteristic sign of the Divinity is manifested in

His infinitude and inexhaustibility, which lead to our inability to exhaust Him by means of our mind. *God is not completely comprehensible to the intellect.* "God cannot be known through reason," says Tolstoy. "It is impossible to understand rationally that God exists and that there is a soul within man; in the same way, it is impossible to understand that there is not God, and that there is no soul within man," he repeats insistently. The first inference, that God is unknowable through reason, brings Tolstoy close to criticism and agnosticism. But does this signify that God is completely unknowable? No, it does not. Although he approaches agnosticism in the unknowability of God through reason, Tolstoy departs from it completely by making *feeling* the instrument of understanding. In this he agrees with the mystics generally, and with the most recent philosophers (for example, Bergson) who make so-called "intuition" the instrument for understanding the absolute. This intuition is in essence what Tolstoy terms "feeling." "*To feel God within oneself is possible and not difficult. To apprehend God, however,* to apprehend what He is, *is impossible and unnecessary.*" "Everyone can *feel* God, but no one can apprehend Him. And so don't try to apprehend Him, but try, while fulfilling His will, to develop an ever more lively *feeling* of Him within yourself" (p. 12).

God cannot be expressed in words and concepts, for if He were expressible then it would no longer be possible for us to strive for Him, there would be no life, and He would not be infinitude. For this reason, "even the pronoun 'He,'" says Tolstoy, "as this is applied to God, already violates in my mind the whole idea of Him. The word 'He' somehow belittles Him." If one wished, one could construct a very close analogy between the role of the intellect in Tolstoy and the so-called "cinematographic mode of thought" of Bergson on the one hand, and between the "feeling" of Tolstoy and the "intuition" of Bergson on the other (Bergson 1912).

And so we do not know God fully, but we do "feel" God fully. We are not able to express Him, but we are fully able to experience Him in feeling (see below).

What, then, are His characteristics which we do know, and which we can express in words? They are *love, intelligence, absolute perfection, truth, and an absolutely wise will.* "Love and intelligence," says Tolstoy, "are those characteristics of God which we recognize in ourselves, but that which He is in Himself we cannot know." "Man needs to love, but it is possible to really love only that in which there is no evil. And for this reason there must exist that which contains no evil: God." Farther on he says: "A man cannot help but feel that something is happening in his life, that he is someone's instrument. But if he is someone's instrument, then there is someone who is working the instrument. *And that someone who is working it is God*" (Tolstoy [1881] 1887, "God," pp. 5, 6, 11). "The supreme will is that which we understand as and name God." "Every truth comes from God."

Such, in short, are the known characteristics of God, and such is Tolstoy's answer to the first question of philosophy. And so *the essence of things is God. We do not completely know Him through the mind, but do know Him completely through feeling (intuition). The known characteristics of God are love, intelligence, absolute perfection, and absolute will.* With this answer Tolstoy has already determined all his answers to the remaining problems of philosophy.

5.

If the essence of things (the logically prior being) is God, then it is clear that our "I" or "soul," as part of everything, is nothing other than part of God. *"The intangible, invisible, immaterial thing which gives life to all that exists we call God. That intangible, invisible, immaterial source, separated by a body from all else and known to ourselves, we call the soul.*" Since the physical My is something which appears to be, it follows that the soul is spiritual. God is an infinite ocean, while the soul is part of that ocean, imprisoned in a material shell (Tolstoy [1881] 1887, "The Soul," p. 3). The entire physical My is constantly changing, in eternal "flux," while the soul alone is indivisible and unchanging, just as God is indivisible and identical to Himself. "A man who has lived a long life has experienced many changes: in the beginning he was an infant, then a child, then an adult, and then an old man. But no matter how much a man changes, he always speaks of himself as 'I.' *And this 'I' within him has always been one and the same*. The very same 'I' was in the infant, and in the adult, and in the old man. *Thus, this changeless 'I' is that which we call the soul*" (p. 3).

As a part of God, the soul possesses all of His characteristics. Thus, like God, it is inexpressible. ("*We cannot say with words what sort of thing this 'I' is, but we know this 'I' better than anything else which we know.*") Just as God presents Himself as the condition and foundation of *every* being, so *for us* the soul presents itself as the condition of all knowledge and being. "We know," says Tolstoy, "that if it were not for this 'I' within us, we would know nothing, nothing in the world would exist for us, and ourselves would not be" (pp. 3-4).

And since, like God, the soul is wise and perfect, it is also, like God, love and will . . . .

Such is Tolstoy's answer to the second question of philosophy, an answer which follows with logical inevitability from his first position on the essence and condition of all being.

From these two positions there naturally follows the resolution of the third problem of philosophy: *How is knowledge of the essence of things possible an und für sich*? How is knowledge of God possible?

Since God is the essence of things, the foundation of being, and since the soul is a part of that being, it follows that the soul and God are one and the same. And if the soul and God are one and the same, then our "I" (the soul) can know God absolutely, because "God lives in me" and "I in Him." We can express neither God nor the soul in words, but we *know* God, immediately feel or experience God . . . . "When I reflect, it is more difficult for me to understand what sort of thing my body is, than what sort of thing my soul is. No matter how near my body may be, it always remains *foreign*, and only the soul is *my own*."

"For God, I am another He. In me He finds that which will always be like Himself" (p. 11). "It is possible to know God only in yourself. If you do not find God in yourself, you will not find Him anywhere" ("God," p. 4).

Because God and the soul are identical, absolute knowledge of God is possible.

This conclusion, as the reader can see, is completely correct logically and is inescapable . . . . Such is the resolution of the third problem of philosophy. . . .

From this last conclusion immediately results what appears, at a glance, to be the paradoxical relation of Tolstoy to science, against which Prof. Isayev particularly protests.

Science studies that which is given to us by the sensory organs, that is, the external world, the world of substantial-material things—and not the foundation of being. The external world, however, as has already been indicated above, is, in Tolstoy's opinion, merely something which seems to be—"our fantasy"—and not something authentically real. (Compare this with the Kantian "appearance.") From this it is clear that the sciences which study this "something which seems to be" cannot be true sciences, but only sciences of "the imaginary" whose values are therefore not great (Bergson 1912).

"If a man thinks that everything he sees around him is an infinite world of just the same sort as he sees, then he is badly mistaken. All that is physical a man knows only because he has one type of sight, hearing, and sense of touch rather than another. *Were these senses different, the whole world would be different.* So it is that we do not know, and cannot know, what sort of thing is the physical world in which we live. The only thing that we truly and fully know is our soul," he says. "*All that is material in this world we cannot know as it really is. We know fully only that which is spiritual within ourselves*" (Tolstoy [1881] 1887, "God," pp. 3, 5).

From these words, it is evident that, above knowledge, Tolstoy places truth, absolute and certain truth. All that is relative and uncertain (as, in his opinion, knowledge of facts and of the external world seem to be) Tolstoy does not value highly. . . . This opinion of his, Prof. Isayev notwithstanding, is neither paradox nor eccentricity, but the inescapable conclusion of his whole philosophical construction. Ordinary science, according to Tolstoy, knows many trifles but does not know that which is important: God, the soul, and the meaning of life. Inasmuch as only the latter are known by us with certainty (feeling), while the former constitute a relative knowledge of the imaginary, it is understandable that the value of the former is quite low. . . . On this point, as on several others, Tolstoy closely approaches Kant and his dualism of the phenomenal and the noumenal.

6.

It remains for us now to characterize Tolstoy's resolution of the fourth problem of philosophy: *the meaning and value of life*. This problem occupies a dominant position in Tolstoy's philosophy, so dominant in fact that it is easy to take him for a pragmatist advancing the principles of utility and suitability for life as the criteria of truth. More attentive study, however, indicates that one cannot speak of Tolstoyan pragmatism, that the question, "How should I live?", as well as its resolution, are the logically inescapable conclusions of the principles of his philosophy previously indicated. . . .

Inasmuch as God is the source of every life, life is nothing other than a manifestation of God, or a part of God striving for unification, with Him. . . . "The life and happiness of a man consist in the ever greater unification of the soul—separated by a body from other souls and from God—with those things from which it is separated" (Tolstoy [1881] 1887, "Life is Happiness," p. 3).

If life is a manifestation of God and a striving for God, and God is happiness, then life also is happiness. Such is Tolstoy's syllogism. "According to false teaching," says Tolstoy, "life in this world is evil, and happiness is attained only in a future life."

"According to true Christian teaching, the goal of life is happiness and this happiness is found here. True happiness is in our hands. Like a shadow, it follows a good life" (pp. 3-4).

Since a part of God is contained in man (the soul), and God is happiness, therefore happiness is within us. Such is the new conclusion of Tolstoy. "God has come into me, and through me He is seeking His own happiness," he says. "And what can the happiness of God be like? Only this, to be Himself." "What greater happiness can there be for you, when you have God and whole world within you?" he asks. (pp. 5-7). "If happiness is not within you yourself, than you will never encounter it," he says, citing Augustine.

From what has been said it is evident as well that the thesis, "*The Kingdom of God is within us," is not a paradox, but an inescapable conclusion from fundamental premises*. And so life is valuable and the supreme blessing. Its meaning consists in an ever greater unification with its first foundation—God. "Human life is a never-ending process of unification of a spiritual being, separated by a body, with that to which it knows itself to be united. Whether a man realizes this or not, whether he wishes it or not, such unification is irresistably accomplished in that condition which we call human life. The difference between those persons who do not understand their vocation and those who wish to live in conformity with it consists in this—that the life of those who do not understand is unending suffering, while the life of those who understand and who fulfill their vocation is unending, ever-increasing happiness" (p. 9). "All suffering is only the My, born of the fact that a man does not recognize his oneness with God, but sees in himself only a physical personality: Ivan, Mavra, and so on. From this, it follows also that while he does not recognize God within himself he becomes weak and unhappy, but when conscious of Him in himself he becomes free, all-powerful and knows no evil." . . . And the more he is aware of Him in himself, the more strongly he strives for Him, the more filled with the meaning his life becomes. This is the highest and ultimate purpose, in relation to which every other purpose becomes relative. Every other purpose, when fulfilled, ceases to be a purpose, says Tolstoy, whereas striving for God never loses its significance, because God is the highest, the ultimate perfection. "One thing alone does not lose its joyous meaning: the consciousness of our movement toward perfection" (p. 10). In other words, the striving for

God is the highest governing principle.

From this principle, in turn, come the following theses:

(a) If the meaning of life consists in unification with God, then unification with other people is unavoidable, because God is contained within them.

Hence, *the general meaning of happiness*. "True blessings are few. Only that is genuinely a blessing and a good which is a blessing and a good for all. Therefore, one ought to desire only that which is in accordance with general happiness. The person whose activity is directed toward that end will find happiness" (p. 11). This thesis is nothing but the famous principle: "Do unto others as you would have them do unto you."

(b) From this, it follows that *unification with God requires not only unification with other people, but also unification with all living things, because they also are a large part of God*. "In our hearts we feel that which we live, and which we call our 'I,' is the very same not only in every person, but even in a dog, a horse, a mouse, and . . . even in a plant." Hence the imperative: "Recognize yourself not only in mankind, but in every living being; don't kill and do not cause suffering and death" ("One Soul in All," p. 7).

(c) Since God is happiness and love, *unification with Him is love*. "This unification occurs as the soul, manifesting itself in love, frees itself more and more from the body." Hence the thesis: "In order to be truly happy only one thing is necessary: love, love all—the good and the evil alike. Love without ceasing, and you will be unceasingly happy." "My life is not my own," writes Tolstoy, "and therefore its purpose cannot be only my own happiness. Its purpose can only be that which is the will of the One who sends me into life. And He wills that all should love one another, the very thing in which my general happiness consists" ("Life Is Happiness," pp. 12-13).

(d) From what has been said comes *Tolstoy's rejection of physical life—a thesis which at first glance is paradoxical*. The body and matter are the boundaries which set us apart from our soul, a part of God, Who is our first principle. They hinder our unification with Him and so must be confined and restricted. Hence the thesis: "The more a man lives for the body, the more he is deprived of true happiness." "Some people seek happiness in power, others in love of learning, in science, while others seek it in pleasure." . . . "Those who have more closely approached true philosophy, however, have understood that general happiness—the object of the striving of all people—must not consist in one of those particular things which can be mastered by only some. On the contrary, true happiness must be that which we can all possess at once, without diminishing it and without jealousy, and must be that which no one can lose through his own will. And happiness is this: happiness is in love" (pp. 14-15).

(e) Equality. Since "the basis of human life is the Spirit of God living within them—one and the same for all people—people cannot possibly be not equal among themselves" ("Inequality," p. 3). "No matter who people may be in themselves, and no matter who their fathers or grandfathers may be, all people are still as equal as two drops of water, because one and the same Spirit of God dwells in them all." "Only those who do not know that God dwells in them can consider some people more important than others" (p. 11).

Here we see a complete parallel between Tolstoy and Kant. For Kant, every man is an end-in-himself and all are equal, not because, as people, they are ends-in-themselves; but rather because every man is an embodiment of intelligent will—the absolute good—and, as such, equal to any other. (See *The Foundations of the Metaphysics of Morals* of Kant.) And the majority of philosophical theories support the principle of equality in the very same way. (Only recently has there been an attempt to support this principle otherwise. See Simmel [1907, pp. 73-88].)

But as has already been shown above, from this it follows that not only people but all living things are equal to one another. (See "One Spirit in All.") From this, the motive for "Is this Really so Necessary" and related publications becomes understandable—as do even such details of Tolstoy's world view as his vegetarianism.

From the very same principle come the motives which Tolstoy brings to *What Is Art*. Every art which is understood by only certain persons and not by all is a false art, because it differentiates humanity, and increases inequality. Therefore it must be rejected (Tolstoy 1898). (This also explains why Tolstoy sets up as his criterion of artistry the contagiousness of moral experience, whose other side is universality and comprehensibility. See his appraisal of the story of Joseph.)

By means of the principle pointed out above, and in no lesser degree by means of the same principle of equality, the reason becomes clear for Tolstoy's rejections of "wisdom" and of the false science which studies a thousand "empty things," discusses them in poorly understood language, and, at the same time, differentiates among people.

From this same principle (derived in turn from other higher

principles) results also his demand for a change to "plain living."

In the same way, one can understand his irreconcilability with teachings such as Nietzsche's superman, the morality of masters and slaves, etc. These are polar positions which cannot be combined.

And the entire activity of Tolstoy the non-artist was a great fulfillment of his own principles, a great equalization of the rich and poor of this world, of the learned and "the ignorant," of masters and slaves. Reflecting the best of what human thought has attained, he converted it into his own philosophical creativity, brought it into union with his entire system, and as a result put these thoughts into a clear and simple statement, equally well understood by the educated and the illiterate.

I will not draw out further details of the world view and conduct of Tolstoy from his fundamental principles. (If one wished, it could be shown.) From what has already been said, it is clear that Tolstoy's philosophy constitutes a single whole in which each part is united with every other and flows logically from what has gone before. And this is seen not only in the fundamental principles, but also in the details of his philosophy and life. *Taking as his fundamental position the thesis that the essence and the foundation of being and life is God, Tolstoy step by step, in a full and systematic way, develops his system. Since the essence of the world is God, then my "I" is also God because I am part of the world. Since God and I are one and the same, I can know Him. If I can know Him, then the significance and value of my life is to strive for Him. Since He is Happiness and Love, my striving for Him is manifested in love. Since He is contained in the "I" of others, and in all living things, then, while striving for Him, I should strive for others and for all living things. And from this thesis, all the principles, the most important of which we have enumerated above, flow of themselves.*

From this it is clear that the criticism of Prof. Isayev can hardly be considered successful. It is possible to disagree with Tolstoy's system, or possible to reject it, but to reject its beauty and logic is hardly permissible. Of course this can be done, but such an attempt of its very nature must be unsuccessful.

7.

In concluding this brief characterization of Tolstoy's philosophical system, I would like to dwell on one further point of his philosophy and its significance for us.

In the realm of artistic creativity, as is well known, there is a distinction between national and general human types. And this distinction concerns not only the types themselves, as products of the artistic creativity of a particular artist; but along with this, it applies to the artists themselves and to the whole character of their creativity as manifestations of nationality, or expressions of the psycho-social tenor of life of the social group or the people.

To a certain degree this phenomenon seems possible also in the realm of philosophy. Above, we have shown that the philosophical is a typical temperament observable through the world view, in contrast to artistic creativity, in which the world view is observable through the temperament. If this is really so, then the very typicality of temperament already presupposes to a certain degree that it cannot be the temperament of an individual but rather the temperament of a group, class or nation . . . . The history of philosophy gives partial support to this phenomenon. . . . Thus, for the Greeks, national philosophy appears in Plato with his firm, "hard" kingdom of ideas, and not in Heraclitus with his "all is flux," because even the "becoming" of Heraclitus speaks of something firm. His "becoming" is not an *uninterrupted* process, but is nothing other than a synthesis of two "firm" concepts: being and nonbeing. Only by combining them was he able to obtain "becoming." Uninterrupted change is not known to the Greeks as a distinctive method.

The very attempt to construct "becoming" speaks of the same "firm" being. (Recall, following Heraclitus, Zeno and his motionless arrow.) The same sort of typical philosophies for the Germans appear in Kant and Hegel with their most abstract and strictly logical systems, and complete renunciation of all empiricism. For the English, on the other hand, the great empiricists Mill and Spencer are characteristic. As the typical French philosopher, everyone would probably cite Comte.

Of course, to some degree this division is relative, but nonetheless, it appears that there is some truth in it.

Approaching Tolstoy from this point of view, we shall perhaps not be mistaken if we designate him and his philosophy as typical of the Russians.

Glancing at our part of history, and, in particular, at the history of the intelligentsia in Russia, we see that it is a continuous self-sacrifice, a constant and incessant "devotion of the soul to its other," a constant bright love not stopping short of any sort of sacrifice.

Along with this, it seems that one could hardly find anywhere a greater rejection of all class and national boundaries than in Russia. . . . Not in vain did Dostoyevsky speak of this, nor V. Solovyov accept it with certain reservations. And so it is not without reason that the entire history of Russian literature appears as continuous heroism, an unending sermon on the ideals of love and truth, a constant "appeal for heroic deeds."

From another vantage point, this love is not rational or artificial, but spontaneous and purely *mystical*. In addition, this mysticism does not appear to be accidental for us. . . . The endless snowy plains, the songs of the blizzard, the long twilight and endless forests together with the sorrow of our life even in ancient times were constructing the soul of the Russian man in a mystical harmony. Consider our popular sayings, epic stories and especially our songs—can one not feel in them, together with grief, a deep secret?

In this connection, could anyone possibly represent Dostoyevsky not as a Russian, but as a German or a Frenchman? Hardly. The Karamazovs and the Raskolnikovs could only have been created by Dostoyevsky, and not by anyone else. We remember also that the major criticism directed at Western science by Solovyov (and before him) was precisely the criticism of excessive rationalism and neglect of "feeling"—that is, of mysticism.

If we keep in mind other similar examples, then perhaps it will not seem strange that these same two features dominate the philosophy of Tolstoy: mysticism and love.

The history of philosophy has known many "essences of the world." Such "essences" have taken the form now of matter, now of spirit, now of will, logic and so forth. But there has hardly been any philosophical system which so sharply and clearly declares the "essence of things" to be God, whose fundamental attribute is a love which knows no boundaries or limits, a love which is not "intellectual" but immediately alive.

Four

SOROKIN, TOLSTOY, AND CIVILIZATIONAL CHANGE

LAWRENCE T. NICHOLS

The following is the Centennial paper read by Lawrence T. Nichols for the 1989 meeting of the International Society for the Comparative Study of Civilizations at Berkeley, California. Nichols, whose translation of Sorokin's "Tolstoy as Philosopher" precedes this chapter, has done excellent research on Sorokin and is an expert on Harvard's Department of Sociology and Social Relations.

Tolstoy was crucial for Sorokin's thought, as this chapter proves. I am greatly indebted to Lawrence T. Nichols for his kind permission to include these two fine essays.

The reasons for this relevancy are manifest in what Sorokin presents as the high content of ideational and idealistic cultures and in his treatment of altruistic creativity. Tolstoy, as interpreted by Sorokin in 1914, reappears without question in the Dynamics *and in Sorokin's Harvard altruism research.*

This paper will argue that Leo Tolstoy had a significant influence on the outlook of Pitirim A. Sorokin, in both a general and specifically sociological sense. With regard to general influence, it will be observed that Tolstoy's impact on Sorokin was lifelong and apparently unique in its importance. With regard to the more specific issue of civilizational change, I shall argue that Sorokin's views were shaped by Tolstoy's approach to altruism and intuitionism. Finally, I will contend that attention to Tolstoy's influence helps us appreciate distinctly Russian elements in Sorokin's thought and in his approach to civilizational change.

1. Tolstoy's General Influence

Sorokin has indicated clearly that Tolstoy was an important influence upon him all his life. Thus, speaking of his childhood, Sorokin (Allen

1963, p. 17) recalled reading Tolstoy along with other famous nineteenth-century Russian writers, and apparently came to regard this literature as the standard by which to judge all others. During his late adolescence and early adult years, Sorokin again read Tolstoy in connection with his immersion in political activism (Allen 1963, pp. 22, 27-28). He was also involved in the student protests that followed Tolstoy's death in 1910 (Sorokin 1963). Shortly thereafter, Sorokin (1914) sketched out Tolstoy's philosophy in an essay, in which he defended Tolstoy's stature as a systematic thinker. Finally, in his work on altruism, Sorokin returned often to the works of Tolstoy, from the time of *The Reconstruction of Humanity* in 1948, to *The Basic Trends of Our Time* in 1964.

With regard to content areas, Tolstoy's influence on Sorokin seems to have been very wide-ranging. As noted above, Sorokin accepted the Tolstoyan doctrine that good art should be ennobling. This point of view was expressed where he asserted that

> Divorced from science and philosophy, religion and ethics, art has grown increasingly vacuous and sterile. . . . It has ceased to elevate its patrons morally or to integrate them mentally. Rather, it demoralizes and enervates them . . . it disseminates the germs of egoism, enmity, strife, and criminality. (Sorokin 1948, p. 123)

A second important area of concordance between Tolstoy and Sorokin is their critical view of modern European science. In his book, *The False Sciences*, Tolstoy had argued that

> All who turn to the science of our day not for the purpose of satisfying idle curiosity, nor to make a living at science, but simply in order to answer direct, simple, vital questions find that science answers for them thousands of complex and learned questions—but not not that one question to which every intelligent person seeks an answer: "What am I, and how am I to live?"

This passage was quoted by Sorokin in his 1914 essay "Leo Tolstoy as a Philosopher" (p. 6). One can readily see resemblances between this position and that formulated by Sorokin in *The Crisis of*

Our Age (1941), *The Reconstruction of Humanity* (1948), and *Fads and Foibles in Modern Sociology* (1956).

The general influence of Tolstoy in the formation of Sorokin's views becomes clearer when we note an apparent psychological *identification* by Sorokin with Tolstoy. This process is best evidenced by the essay "Leo Tolstoy as a Philosopher" (1914), where Sorokin serves as Tolstoy's advocate, defending Tolstoy's claim as a philosopher from critical assaults. Such identification is also suggested much later in Sorokin's career, where his "prophetic" demeanor resembles that of Tolstoy in the latter's "post-conversion" phase. The later Tolstoy may thus have provided an important role model for the later Sorokin, as a dissident intellectual who persevered in his teachings and moral exhortations despite condemnation and misunderstanding.

It is therefore not surprising that Tolstoy's strongest influence on Sorokin appears to have been in the area of religion and ethics. Following his famous conversion at about the age of fifty, Tolstoy gradually developed a distinctive formulation of Christian dogmas that ultimately resulted in his excommunication by the Russian Orthodox Church (Troyat 1980). The Tolstoyan system retains a strong emphasis on Christian ethics, but rejects other tenets of traditional Christianity, especially that of the divinity of Jesus. This viewpoint—which resembles a Russian Transcendentalism or Unitarianism—seems to have been shared by Sorokin (1956a).

The Tolstoyan treatment of religion and ethics also included a strong emphasis on intuitionism, which became characteristic of Sorokin's works in the last twenty years of his life. Evidence for this influence is provided in Sorokin's early essay on Tolstoy's philosophy (Sorokin 1914, p. 10), in which he stated that

> Although he approaches agnosticism in the unknowability of God through reason, Tolstoy departs from it completely by making *feeling* the instrument of understanding. In this he agrees with the mystics generally, and with the most recent philosophers (for example, Bergson) who make so-called "intuition" the instrument for understanding the absolute.

Fifty years later, writing of "the role of the supraconscious in discoveries and creativity," Sorokin (1964, p. 33) again cited Tolstoy as an important thinker who recognized "intuitional truths as the basis of all the mathematical, logical, and sensory-observational verities in all fields of human cognition and creativity." Sorokin's "integral theory of cognition" appears broader than Tolstoyan epistemology, but it grants a privileged place to intuition and acknowledges Tolstoy's influence in so doing.

Thus, the general influence of Tolstoy seems to have been unique with regard to Sorokin's personal outlook, his published theories, and his role as dissident intellectual. Other important influences on Sorokin—including especially Aristotle, Jesus, Leo Petrazhitsky, and Sri Aurobindo—did not have the same impact over a period of some seventy years, nor across a comparably broad range of issues. The similarities of perspective become clearer when we realize that the term used by Sorokin to describe his outlook, that of "conservative Christian anarchist," applied equally well to Tolstoy.

2. Tolstoy's Influence on Sorokin's View of Change

During the final thirty years of his long career, Sorokin developed and tenaciously defended the view that only creative altruism could provide a way out of the crisis faced by Western civilization. Tolstoy is a significant influence in the formation of this view. This means also that Tolstoy was influential in shaping Sorokin's commitment to nonviolence in responding to the contemporary crisis. With regard to nonviolence, moreover, it appears that the Tolstoyan influence on Sorokin was reaffirmed and reinforced by the activism of Gandhi. We shall consider each of these points in turn.

Both Sorokin and Tolstoy believed strongly that Western civilization was confronted by a crisis of major historical significance, which could only be resolved through the creation of a cultural and social life based upon altruism. Thus, in *The Kingdom of God Is Within You* (originally published in 1905), Tolstoy argued that

> Neither man nor humanity can in their motion turn back. The social, family, and political life-conceptions have been outlived by men, and it is necessary to go ahead and accept the higher life-conception, which indeed is being done now. (Tolstoy 1961, p. 117)

Refusal to accept the necessity of cultural change, according to

Tolstoy, accounted for much of the conflict and pain of the era. As he asserted,

> Humanity . . . knows the teaching which ought to be put at the foundation of the life of his new age, but from inertia continues to hold on to the previous forms of life. From this lack of correspondence between the life-conception and the practice of life there arises a series of contradictions and sufferings, which poison our life and demand its change. (Tolstoy 1961, p. 118)

Several decades later, Sorokin presented a strikingly similar diagnosis and prognosis in *The Reconstruction of Humanity* (1948), which seems to parallel Tolstoy's *Kingdom of God.* Before discussing altruism, Sorokin dismissed other strategies for solving the historical crisis, including political, economic, scientific, educational, and religious approaches (see chaps. 1-3). None of these, Sorokin argued, could address the violence of the period of crisis. He concluded that "such plans either neglect the decisive factor of altruism and love . . . or are unable to make the overt behavior of persons and groups . . . more altruistic . . . . Whatever the other prerequisites of a creative and lasting peace may be, it cannot be achieved without a substantial increase of love, sympathy, and free cooperation in the overt relationships of persons and groups" (Sorokin 1948, pp. 53-54).

This view was reaffirmed in *The Ways and Power of Love,* where Sorokin argued that

> Only the power of unbounded love practiced in regard to *all human beings* can defeat the forces of interhuman strife, and can prevent the pending extermination of man by man on this planet. Without love, no armament, no war, no diplomatic machinations, no coercive police force, no school education, no economic or political measures, not even hydrogen bombs can prevent the pending catastrophe. (1954, p. ii)

As he developed this perspective in *Ways and Power of Love,* Sorokin placed explicit emphasis on Tolstoy and his doctrines. In a key passage, Sorokin (1954, p. 138) cited Tolstoy's "insistence on the unconditional and incessant following of the rules of the Sermon on the Mount in our behavior" as "the only way towards building a harmonious, happy, and creative human universe." This statement was followed by seven citations from different portions of Tolstoy's work *The Law of Love and the Law of Violence*. These included Tolstoy's statement that wars and revolutions (that is, byproducts of civilizational crisis) "will disappear, not with the aid of external means, but thanks only to the calls of conscience of men who have awakened to the truth."

With regard to, finally, the "Russianness" of Sorokin's perspective on civilizational change, the influence of Tolstoy appears again to have been important. This is best revealed in Sorokin's 1914 essay *Leo Tolstoy as a Philosopher*, where he characterizes Tolstoy's perspective as "typical of the Russians" (Sorokin 1914, p. 22). The crucial elements of Russian civilization captured by Tolstoy were said to be two: mysticism and love. The same elements were frequently cited in Sorokin's later works by a series of critics who interpreted his approach as unscientific and anti-modern—but who generally did not recognize an underlying Russian point of view in these formulations.

3. Conclusion

I have argued that, despite his enormous erudition and unquestioned originality, Pitirim A. Sorokin was influenced by Leo Tolstoy more than by almost any other thinker. Tolstoy's influence was found to be very broad and to have continued throughout Sorokin's life, from childhood to the writings of his last decade. Particular emphasis was placed upon Tolstoy's influence on Sorokin's interpretation of sociocultural change, especially with respect to "the crisis of our age" and its resolution. Even on the level of everyday occupational behavior, Tolstoy was found to provide an important role model for Sorokin as dissident, intellectual, and prophet of the new age of altruism. The Tolstoyan influence, and the concordance of perspectives, were capsulized in Sorokin's description of his perspective as "conservative Christian anarchism"—a motto that applies equally well to Tolstoy.

To be sure, both points of view emerged from broader movements of thought, especially those reflected in the "Slavophilism" of nineteenth-century Russia. Consequently, a reading of Sorokin that is alert to the influence of Tolstoy recasts his work as part of an ongoing dialogue between representatives of European-American civilization, and their counterparts from a cultural tradition that straddles both Europe and Asia.

Five

SOROKIN vs. AMERICAN THOUGHT

This chapter is based on the first paper I read for the International Society for the Comparative Study of Civilizations at Northridge, California in 1979. I am indebted to the then American editor for Sociologia Internationalis, *Joseph Ford, for his suggestions, and to the journal's publisher, Dunker and Humblot, for permission to reprint it here in revised form.*

The volcano metaphor I borrowed from Theodor von Laue, though colorful enough in its own way, anticipates the "radial contrariety" notion I introduced ten years later at the meeting in Berkeley. The cultural contrast between Sorokin and his American colleagues was the heart of this essay, and the paper by Tibbs was perhaps its greatest stimulus.

Appreciations of Pitirim A. Sorokin's work had their limits among Americans, since he and his critics worked from such diverse philosophical backgrounds. Their selections from, and interpretations of, the data of Western civilization are very different. Sorokin's development will be treated first. Following observations on the American scholarly scene, the response to his theory of the "cultural supersystems" will be discussed. To examine this cultural gap is to raise the question of how Sorokin's philosophy of culture should be regarded today. This issue can be treated in light of the notion that sociology, when it looks at culture, is close to philosophy. It is time to see the Golden Age of American philosophy in a joint perspective with Sorokin, whose hiring by Harvard is midway between James's welcoming of Dewey's "Chicago School" and the present. Lastly, remarks upon the spectrum of American sociology, and Sorokin's stances toward it, will conclude the discussion.

1. Sorokin's Background

Despite Sorokin's belief in the similarity between American and European cultural trends (Sorokin 1941, pp. 280ff.), one can claim that there is a gap that yawns as one moves east. Sorokin's thought reflects his Russian origins and revolutionary experiences. He says so in his autobiography, referring to his worldview in the early 1920s as a reversal of Westernizing liberal progressivism (Sorokin 1963, pp. 204-5). He had entered politics from a peasant background and joined the non-Marxist Social Revolutionaries. Once a student in Petrograd, he studied Comtean thought with enthusiasm. Ultimately, however, he was driven toward an anti-political position.

It is remarkable how Sorokin changes his intellectual direction. Before beginning revolutionary agitation and plunging into social science at the University of Petrograd, his thinking had been religious and idealistic. His linking with Social Revolutionaries showed identification with peasants rather than with urban workers (Sorokin 1963, p. 44). There are reasons for his changing from a positivist direction. He came to distrust Western liberalism because of Kerensky's vacillations and his feelings that Russia was abandoned by the Allies (Sorokin 1963, pp. 150-51). Next, he opposed the Leninist rule. His activities from 1918 until being expelled four years later were "counter-revolutionary." For instance, his book, *Hunger as a Factor in Human Affairs*, (1922) was burned by the Bolsheviks. Sorokin's escape was a near thing; the bureaucrat who issued his exit visa was severely rebuked. Friends mailed a message; "Grandmother was sorry she was unable to give you her final embrace."

Furthermore, the conditions for Sorokin's reversal lie deep in the Russian culture and heritage. Disillusion with revolution, like Dostoyevsky's, found historical support in his *The Sociology of Revolution* (1925). As he idolized Tolstoy, he participated in demonstrations at the sage's death in 1910. Tolstoyan notions arise in his deep dislike of all establishments, his distaste for modern art and culture, his "conservative Christian anarchism," his view of secular leaders as "instrumentalities and puppets" of the crisis, his advocacy of "total and universal disarmament," and echoes of lay monasticism in the Harvard Center for the Study of Creative Altruism.

There is also the Slavophilism found in *Social Philosophies of an Age of Crisis*. There Danilevsky is respectfully treated, along with the Balt Walter Schubart and with Nicholas Berdyaev (Sorokin 1950, pp. 22-44). Sorokin's mature thought, given full expression from the 1930s on, is comparable to that of Berdyaev, except that Berdyaev had first gone through a Marxist to a religious and idealist phase, while Sorokin started from a religious background and proceeded through Westernized positivism back again toward his "integral" worldview. Both men attack what they see as questionable modern values, although neither is simply reactive. Sorokin affirmed the continuing value of his rather positivist *System of Sociology*, published in 1920. Berdyaev nourished, as did Sorokin, a lasting suspicion of Western capitalism. In short, both thinkers sublimate parallel Western values within their anti-Western and anti-Marxist critiques.

Sorokin also discusses and draws upon Spengler, and argues for Danilevsky's influence upon that thinker. The other four social philosophers treated are Toynbee, Northrop, Kroeber, and Schweitzer. Of those, Kroeber is charged with sensate limitations, and Schweitzer with voluntarism; evidently the latter's Western European *Aufklärung* sympathies were alien to Sorokin. Toynbee's Augustinizing of Gibbon and Thucydides is not so distant from Sorokin's Platonizing of Comte. In both cases an idealistic reversal of secular optimism takes place. Northrop's philosophy of culture is qualified, but not rejected entirely.

On the whole, Sorokin treats both anti-Westernizing reactions and internal revolts within Western Europe more tenderly than other views. Beyond this, all the writers examined are highly praised for seeking, unlike more empirical social scientists, macrosociological answers in the study of civilization.

To look at the tensions expressed in the West/East contrast, we may appeal to a very handy metaphor. Theodore von Laue, in his fine book *The Global City* (1969), suggests that industrial progress originating in England and France spilled over across Europe, and that that powerful current was like the eruption of a volcano with its lava flowing irresistibly and destructively down the mountain slopes.

Powerful ambivalent responses were then put into play, such as a German romantic nationalist reaction against all the Enlightenment and its works. Likewise, we can read the Slavophil movement and Tolstoy's work, not to mention Danilevsky's and Sorokin's own writing, as a still later "downslope" rebuttal to Westernization. It is in this respect that scholars can see Sorokin's major work as a response to a drastic encounter with Westernization, primarily with the Marxists in his own country, and afterwards with secular liberals in this country.

At this point an observation might usefully be ventured about the frequently anti-political Russian disposition. Sorokin, as was seen, abjured the more overt sort of political activity in 1918. While circumstances forced activism upon him, this was also in tune with the normally disillusioning Russian political experience, where such disaffiliation is felt the more acutely the farther one goes downslope.

Tolstoy is himself paradigmatic, and he had a strong influence upon *Power and Morality* (1959). In Sorokin's own case, he continued to renounce overt politics—for all of the scholarly contributions he made toward both political science and the critique of Communism—in *Hunger as a Factor in Human Affairs*, *The Sociology of Revolution*, *Social Mobility* (1927), and *Man and Society in Calamity* (1942). The level of abstraction in his sociology facilitates a rising above immediate political issues, even while denouncing all "sensate power elites."

Yet, any temptation to say his approach is one of "Plague on both your houses" should be resisted. Sorokin engaged most actively in protests, warnings and scolding of both East and West, anxious as he was lest "sensate power elites" blow us all up. In 1944 he published a book, following much of the line of Danilevsky, entitled *Russia and the United States*. In it, he discounted the idea of conflict between America and Russia. Events showed that to be hopeful thinking on his part. His later observations increased his disgust with the follies of politics. This repeated withdrawal and adverse judgment upon politics is continuous in tone with his retirement from political activity in 1918.

The most controversial aspect of Sorokin's "downslope" reaction is found in his reading of "cultural supersystems." A late statement about this is included in the Introduction to *Sociological Theories of Today*, where he sets forth this basis for criticism of current theories.

> Besides these vast cultural systems [religion, language, fine arts, law and ethics, politics and economics] there are still vaster cultural unities that each. . . is based upon. . . certain ultimate principles. . . . The vastest of these are supersystems whose major premises or ultimate principles concern the nature of the ultimate true reality or the ultimate true value. Three main consistent answers have been given . . . . One is: "The true, ultimate reality-value is sensory. Beyond it there is no other reality or any other nonsensory value." This premise and the gigantic supersystem built upon it is called the sensate supersystem.
>
> Another answer. . . is: "The true, ultimate reality-value is the Manifold Infinity, which contains all differentiation and which is infinite qualitatively and quantitatively. The finite human mind cannot grasp

> it or define it or describe it adequately in its infinite plenitude. . . . Only by a very remote approximation can we discern three main aspects in it: the rational or logical, the sensory, and the superational-supersensory". . . . This typically three-dimensional conception of the ultimate and the supersystem built upon it is described as idealistic or integral.
>
> Each of these three supersystems embraces in itself the corresponding type of the vast systems already described. (1966, pp. 23-24)

An origin for Sorokin's cultural supersystem can be suggested. Auguste Comte wielded his "law of three stages" (theological, metaphysical, and positive) chiefly as a publicist's mnemonic against religion and prescientific philosophy. Sorokin reversed the polarity of that schematism in terms of popularized Platonism, attacking Sophistic empiricism. Evidence for the correspondence is that Comte's theological stage anticipates Sorokin's "ideational" phase of culture, that the metaphysical stage matches the "idealistic" phase, and that the "positive" stage, the culmination of intellectual progressivism, is denigrated by Sorokin as "sensate." The three stages under the Platonic reversal gave Sorokin, a former publicist himself, a frame of reference that is memorable, if not entirely convincing, to Westerners. To this framework he brought reams of data. While at various points qualifying it, he kept coming back to the schema as a basis for his preachments. Though admitting the strength of sensate culture from the Renaissance through the nineteenth century, he held that empirical and utilitarian assumptions have now decayed.

From a downslope angle, Sorokin heralded a transfiguration of the West from upslope down, even while pointing out attendant dangers. The mnemonic linking his advocacy and his science depended on "cultural supersystems," the working out of which elicited cultural super-revolutions. In one respect, Sorokin looked for a super-counter-revolution, given his restoking of flames from old "Battles of Books." He hinted that yesterday's losers are tomorrow's winners. He cheered for Ancients, realists, humanists, theologians, conservatives, rationalists, and men of faith against the reigning Moderns, nominalists, scientists, empiricists, and skeptics. That suggests too much of a reaction, however, since his predicted transfiguring of culture cannot return us to a *status quo ante*. Even as qualified, this theory was too unattractive for many Amercian colleagues.

Sorokin's forceful critique was massive. He had plotted the direction of *The Social and Cultural Dynamics* before his appointment to Harvard, after teaching at Minnesota from 1924 to 1930 (Sorokin 1963, pp. 235-37). When Harvard officials made their offer to Sorokin, one suspects that, though some of his ideas were manifest, they could not have anticipated such an assault upon "sensate culture," whether of Marxist or capitalist brands. As it happened, Academe in America took a jaundiced view of Sorokin's thesis (Tibbs 1943, pp. 473-80).

2. The American Reaction

Despite such aspects of American life and culture as nativist reactions against immigrants, populist revolts against Wall Street, or Southern agrarian protests against commercialism, the downslope reaction metaphor, taken from von Laue, can never fit any American as well as it does Sorokin. Why not? America, because of a number of temporary advantages (natural resources and the Atlantic ocean), was not a helpless victim of developments forced upon her. Problems were felt as local ones; even the most aggravated nativist was optimistic in the long run about political solutions here. It was less likely that professional scholars would be other than optimistic about our problems. The tone of Golden Age philosophy and Chicago sociology had been well set before World War I.

The American self-image was progressive, and complacent. Americans prided themselves on having made a fresh start, on having broken with what they took as clumsy European traditions. While Sorokin saw them as the tag-end of a collapsing Western culture slated for an ideational transfiguration, they saw themselves as liberated from heavy baggage under which they believed Europeans, Sorokin among others, still labored (Tibbs 1943, p. 477).

One sample of a cultural clash with progressive humanism was a debate between Sorokin and Henry Aiken, attended by myself in 1950. Aiken was a disciple of R.B. Perry, who'd been a disciple of William James, and he shared a sympathy for ethical naturalism and a confidence in science and liberal institutions. Aiken was the best platform artist Harvard philosophers fielded at the time. Yet, not only did Harvard philosophers and Sorokin have no meeting of minds, despite all of them working in Emerson Hall, this particular debate was no contest. Sorokin gave a more powerful presentation, and incidentally, the audience's attention had first been distracted from Aiken's speech, while Sorokin had been swinging his snow-booted leg faster and faster until his turn at the podium. By the way, earlier in his life Sorokin had been the Social Revolutionaries' choice to debate Trotzky, so his debating skills were forged in a rougher forum than Cambridge.

Students were drawn to Sorokin, yet their backgrounds and goals were filters, affecting who was drawn, and how. I myself came from a border state, had some agrarian, populist, and New Deal sympathies-excluding those of urban radicalism—and was both a Quaker-influenced Methodist and a student of the humanities. An acquaintance of mine, a business-oriented Social Relations major, never once mentioned Sorokin, but a community-service oriented New Englander recommended Sorokin's course. On the other hand, an elder kinsman, a student of economics and the law, normally quite soft-spoken, referred to Sorokin as a "windbag." What of students in the social sciences? Not only were they subject to countervailing influences, but any with activist ambitions for guiding capitalist enterprise, or the welfare-state, or for heroically transforming either, must have been disconcerted by Sorokin's anti-secular, anti-sensate, pessimism. In fact, despite my unworldly major in English, I had doubts about the "supersystems." Yet, though amused at times, as at the debate with Aiken, I took Sorokin seriously enough to pursue a study of his thought in a graduate course at Columbia.

Though Sorokin's thought as a whole was not devoid of popular appeal, this did not mean his theory of cultural supersystems was embraced by American academics. In fact, while the *Dynamics* was widely reviewed, it gained a far better reputation at the popular level than at the professional.

For example, a distinguished historian of ideas and disciple of John Dewey, J.H. Randall, Jr., once suggested in a review of the *Dynamics* that its author could not be serious (Randall 1937, p. 922). Such exasperation may be comprehended in terms of Sorokin's simplistic classification and failure to take philosophy as having a directionality given by the development of science and of political institutions. He had little real understanding of, or appreciation for, the Kantian heritage. That helps account for his refusal to draw upon Cambridge pragmatism. His "integralism" is rooted in a Russian Neo-Platonic legacy, tinged by Hegelianism, and his epistemology conflates Comte's crude positivism with religious mysticism. His schema for philosophical positions is especially one-dimensional and rather polemical where concerned with the alleged "sensate" phases.

As to the responses in Sorokin's field, sociologists themselves had mixed views as to his contributions. Consider Robert E. Park's review of the first three volumes of the *Dynamics*. There, the frame of reference and the use of statistics is not treated too favorably, however amiable, perhaps jocular, the reviewer's mood (Parks 1941, pp. 904 ff.). The sort of general sociology which Sorokin favored ("sociology in the grand manner") was increasingly out of fashion with specializing professionals. Sorokin even suggested in various places, including his presidential address to the American Sociological Association, that contemporary empiricist approaches in sociology marked a declining "sensate" phase in science (Sorokin 1956).

At times, the distance professional colleagues put between themselves and Sorokin was great. One illustration was the affair of C. Wright Mills's *The Sociological Imagination*. Sorokin, and his sympathizer F. R. Cowell, both mentioned Mills's appreciative letter to Sorokin about *Fads and Foibles in Sociology* and Mills's forgetting to give Sorokin any credit in his own book (Sorokin 1963, p. 297). Friedrichs, by contrast, detaching himself from Sorokin's polemics, then deplores the similarity of the two books (Friedrichs 1970, p. 31), while still remarking favorably on Mills's version. Two observations should be made: Friedrichs trivializes Sorokin's crusade, and secondly, he reveals the point that the borrower Mills had more credibility in the field than did Sorokin. The explanation for this must be that Sorokin was seen as having gone too far with unassimilable ideas. That was the core of the cultural clash, which cropped up on all fronts. But probably the one response most frustrating to Sorokin was being ignored, so provocations were better than silence.

The clash came to focus in a contest between Sorokin and Talcott Parsons. Sorokin unfolded temporally extensive cultural horizons, while discounting modernity. A typically American optimism marked Parsons, whose functionally wide horizons encompassed, with satisfaction, the interactions of modernity. Parsons mediated for American sociology great European theories, bringing them to bear upon the American concern with action. He was in tune with upslope phenomena and competent to produce a marketable form of sociology for American social engineering.

Parsons, it must be said, de-emphasized Sorokin's ideas, and at times, Sorokin took badly what he called the "amnesia" shown by "new Columbuses" (Sorokin 1956, p. 322f.). This might be extenuated somewhat, first, in terms of what Parsons took to be "protosociology" and common coinage in the profession, and secondly, since such ideas might be seen as reaching a better, locally acceptable "convergence" than that given by Sorokin. That "structural-functionalism" later fell, in its turn, into some disrepute was due less to Sorokin than to other factors, such as dissident turmoil.

3. On Bridging the Gap

Here I may treat Sorokin on cultural transmission as somehow self-referential.

"If the two cultures (of departure and infiltration) differ, the migrating cultural phenomenon changes, and the greater the difference of the two cultures, of persons or of groups, the more it changes" (Sorokin 1950, p. 303).

The problem is set for sociology and philosophy. Can the cultural gap between Sorokin and his American critics be narrowed by dialectically transforming the most resistant ideas? The American academic mind, often instructed by Sorokin, has been perplexed by his larger purposes. Were such perplexity diminished, perhaps large questions could once more be raised, such as those regarding civilization, which were fiercely pursued by Sorokin and, in sharp contrast, so studiously ignored by empiricists. I suspect that the truth lies somewhere between Sorokin and his various critics.

The question calls for mediation. This, of crucial concern to culturologists, is the problem with supersystems; here the difference can be split between Sorokin and his critics. It can be addressed on the supposition that the "supersystems" are themselves to be dropped, while many of their appearances may be saved. Maquet's fair-minded analysis and Cowell's advocacy do not protect Sorokin's more sweeping views against criticism (Maquet 1951, chaps. 7-10), as shown by Robert Nisbet's rejection of theories of immanental change (Nisbet 1960, pp. 275-82).

In Sorokin's defense, the reality of systems, cultural and social, may be asserted beneath the level of "supersystems." Such is assured by *de facto* agreements upon ways of life and thought embodied in symbolic and institutional terms. Such consensus is not found for any total all-inclusive system. In various qualifications, Sorokin implied as much, but without drawing the conclusion (Sorokin 1966, pp. 415-17).

An all-encompassing ideal of cultural unity could be projected by members of some ruling group, but such an ideal has such practical limits that it does not deserve a totalizing reification. The actuality of a supersystem, contrasted with the ideal, might be a *modus vivendi* among its subsystems. At one far point, society is controlled by religious institutions, at the other, by secular ones. A *modus vivendi* is more of a compromise than a normative way of life. (Sorokin, in his celebration of the ideational, had overlooked the religious/secular conflict of Western European Middle Ages because of his Byzantine-Russian heritage.) Americans, from their often-Protestant standpoint, could never see the Middle Ages as idyllic, nor as exemplifying purely one "supersystem."

Spengler's term "physiognomy" may be given a modest use, as alluding to the outward appearance of the actuality constituted by the *modus vivendi*. During "sensate" stages, while secular institutions are producing well, "conspicuous consumption" and worldly incentives are highlighted. Religious values do not dominate. In "overripe" phases elites lose their grip. Overreaching characterizes their vainglory and promotions toward their constituencies. Not all of Sorokin's analyses and indictments were untimely, given human excesses.

We now draw up our balance sheet. Generally, American scholars ignore symbolic systems and normative forms of life in favor of voluntarist action. Disliking the latter emphasis, Sorokin favors the former. Yet, the American stress upon individual acts is not without acknowledgment of its standards. William James's "live options" seem to be nothing other than ways of life and thought believed worthy of approbation. Yet, the later anti-formal, empiricist distrust of "cultural lag" and of the "quest for certainty," typical of the Chicago School, created a vacuum to pull in more structured reactions. At Chicago occurred the Great Books struggle and the anti-empiricist arguments of the political scientist Leo Strauss. As for radical reactions, everywhere there were challenges by Marxists, to which Sorokin's testimony was one notable counter-challenge.

But common ground can be claimed between Harvard thought and Sorokin's, despite his partial alienation from Kant, who had given Protestantism a midslope accommodation to modernity. Cambridge Pragmatists, "the children of Kant," carried this accommodation further, as did Max Weber and Karl Jaspers at European midslope. Kantians usefully remind us that an act is not only the act of an organism, as naturalists say, it is the proximate center of meaning, where social "forms of life" are received and initiated. Individual actions and correlative normative patterns are to be affirmed jointly (Duncan 1969, p. 279). Where pragmatists stressed the former, Sorokin emphasized the latter. In truth, scholarship has to work from both sides. Despite Sorokin's *simpliste* approach, he does bring out strikingly what tended to be tacit in Golden Age individualism.

Let me sum up these remarks. Supersystems, with their alleged immanental causality, are to be dropped while *modi vivendi* among subsystems are taken to present "physiognomies" at some points like Sorokin's supersystems. Still, the superorganic, and even the "supraconscious," are worth affirming.

4. Sorokin Rejected

Such mediations may be pursued in a cool hour, well after the cultural clash which left Sorokin so isolated. There was no major phase in the development of American sociology to which Sorokin's culturology could be readily attached.

One can list four phases that are roughly chronological, while overlapping in their antecedents and development. There is the Chicago School influenced by Golden Age philosophers; next, from the mid-thirties on, there emerged what became "structural-functionalism" with its Parsonsian character; thirdly, an anti-functionalist emphasis on conflict took place, this slipping into a "dialectical paradigm" detectably neo-Marxist; and lastly, there is the post-war computerized, statistical research emphasis. Sorokin fits into none of these slots, partly because he gloried in anti-secularism.

Sorokin's defiance of establishment views seems to reach a height in his claim that cultural supersystems are causally determinative. A positive construal of this, where ideational and idealistic systems are at issue, is that Sorokin calls forth an antidote to any historicist relativism that arises from normative acculturation. Inherited points of reference brought by religious and philosophical traditions (ideational and idealistic) are influential upon the ways in which we coordinate our values, including short-range "ideological" ones. The voice of God, or of Reason, which engages" integralist" responses, goes beyond parochialism, since inherited traditions antedate temporary group interests. With the long view, a corrective is provided against bias. Sorokin's insight into the integrating role of sublimated myth, though cast as social science in an oscillating pattern, accounts for his dislike of "sensate" theories that neither acknowledge nor promote correctives for worldly capitalist or communist ideologies. A parallel scientific disguise was given to religious and ethical notions by the founder of Harvard psychology, William James. Wisdom in any guise being very difficult to come by, James and Sorokin have earned our appreciation.

PART TWO

CULTURAL SYSTEMS

Pitirim A. Sorokin, Minnesota, ca. 1929-1930

Six

WORLDVIEWS AND PERSPECTIVISM

This chapter seeks a viable perspectivism and, by doing so, implicates Sorokin's integralist theory of value. Why? Both nihilism and dogmatic exclusivism are unacceptable to Sorokin, and any viable perspectivism must steer between those extremes. To reinforce the essential point, any historical sociology or comparative cross-cultural enterprise that must take many values seriously, as does Sorokin's integralism, has to be perspectival. Pluralism and perspectivism do not imply nihilism, which is a sociocultural pathology characteristic of supersystemic decay according to Sorokin's diagnosis.

"Perspectivism" is a term in good and bad repute among various scholars. A need arises to defend it with care and discrimination, if all is not to collapse into nihilism. Any defense must be adapted to articulated "worldviews," themselves properly acknowledged as perspectival. Naturally, all thought, as well as perception and theory of knowledge, has to be perspectival from the bottom up. Philosophy has to start out somewhere, and every "somewhere" is situationally conditioned. That is surely the case. But does that open the door to reading serious thought as art, or as "aestheticism," or to explaining away in their entirety philosophical positions through Neo-Freudian psycho-history or Neo-Marxist sociology of knowledge? (Sorokin had personally regarded both Marx and Freud as disastrous influences.)

Let me now divide the question, and confront the insidious aestheticist's challenge. Nietzschean "perspectivism" can be interpreted in free-wheeling aesthetic terms. The philosopher who stresses "traditions," for example, Alisdair MacIntyre, seemingly regards the "perspectivist" very much as if he is a bored tourist being dragged past endless vistas—all these viewings capable of being surveyed, but not of being judged better or worse, or as true or false, by the tourist encountering the proferred perspectives as totally indifferent, while he goes by in a virtual stupor.

MacIntyre's multi-traditionalism, with all its lengthy and acute analyses, might tempt a person to call him a perspectivist of sorts, but that would not do. He overstresses the separate status of mainline traditions, downplaying their manifold dialectical crossings. To resolve perceived difficulties with modern traditions, such as those he finds in empiricist liberalism, he reaches back to an older line from Aristotle through Aquinas. His is not so much a dialectical perspectivism then, as a disguised mono-traditionalism. (The difficulty MacIntyre finds in liberalism, its alleged basis in bare raw preferences, is not unlike Sorokin's critique of overripe sensate culture; but John Stuart Mill and even William James gave room for culturated, hence normative, preferences, and the guidance of the wise. So healthy sensate culture is a dialectical product from idealism and empiricism, as in Mill's mediation between Bentham and Coleridge. Sorokin's integralism also was itself mediated, though between older cultural types.)

Yet the Hegelian "Absolute Spirit" yields worldviews which claim truth as well as the value of art. What distinctions can be drawn here to save perspectivism from relativisms of a nihilist cast and recent types of deconstructionist irony? One good clue is "aesthetic distance." Let us take art as exercising human recognitional and responsive capacities, as opposed both to utilizing them in actuality and to encompassing the whole range of actualities, or attempting to do so, as do religious and philosophical systems. Art simply contemplates ranges of possibilities, thereby exercising human capacities. Worldviews are something else again.

How? Worldviews variously invoke the self, drawing the recipient and incipient of culture into some orientation, giving the self direction by organizing ways of life and thought. Orientative strategies are thus brought into play as world-views. In sharp contrast, art evokes aspects of the self to awaken capacities quite elemental to ways of thought and life. The self is not thereby committed to any ordering of thought or of policies; so "aestheticism" misreads the nature of worldviews.

To subsume philosophy and religion under art is clearly to void a crucial distinction, even if "there are no absurdities that are not found in the books of the philosophers" and even if our history had not given us unparalleled retrogressions in religious life. Ideologies, as well as religions and philosophies, have been subsumed under "worldviews," and this creates difficulties in science. (Marxist ideologies are universally in crisis, and "capitalism" often works out to be a cover story for activities of a doubtful nature.)

For the second step of defending perspectivism as non-nihilistic, one can claim that some perspectives are better than others, and that less acceptable perspectives, whether religious, philosophical, or ideological, may arise from untoward influences upon their proponents. Often enough, persons unfortunately let themselves be carried away in their thinking. That may well have happened through neglecting considerations they should have let themselves attend to, whether current influences, or lasting influences from the past as memories or traditions. At times, to unleash the vengeance of the psycho-historian or the sociologist of knowledge is not unfair, but the selective dismissal of unfortunate perspectives does not eliminate the good odds that a range of perspectives may come as well-grounded. In short, perspectives may serve sociocultural functions, all of which are reasonable, so that perspectives A, B, and C approximate soundness, no one of them necessarily doing the full job. Each may be preferred, in R. G. Collingwood's phrase, as an "interim report," even in the permanent absence of any final report. At its best, a perspective, however tentative, must often be taken seriously.

In view of some current interest in "systematic pluralism," let us scan the ranges of worldview types to see what, if any, morals may be drawn. Karl Jaspers emphasized the incompleteness, one-sidedness, and partiality of objectified systems, whether naturalism, intellectualism, mysticism, idealism or (secular) existentialism. He finds that distortions arise from taking one or even two aspects presented to us as being exhaustive. Furthermore, Jaspers's "periechontology" in no way advocated a synthesis of such systems. So he at best distrusts "isms" claiming finality, while his masterwork *Philosophie* scans aspects of the Comprehensive with subtlety and grace.

Wilhelm Dilthey gave a sympathetic account of psychological rootages of naturalisms, idealisms of freedom, and objective idealisms. He did not recommend one preferred type from these, but claimed that perennial motivations give rise to these standard sorts, and also to mixes. William James had sympathized with both "tough-minded" empiricists and "tender-minded" idealists, and he proposed a synthesis in terms of his own pragmatism. Ralph Barton Perry added a fourth type, realism, to James's naturalism, idealism, and pragmatism. Royce favored objective idealism above mysticism, realism, and critical rationalism. (Critical rationalism he ascribed to James as well as to the great forerunner, Kant.) But Royce is out of the line of apostolic succession from James through Perry down to some contemporary metaphilosophers.

Morals can be drawn from all those metaphilosophical accounts. Perspectives derive from differing sources and serve diverse ends. Their pretenses of finality and completeness are subject to doubt. The co-existence of contrasting schools suggest their incompleteness, and recurring dissatisfactions with them lead toward an ideal movement of unification, despite falling short of the goal. The transcendence of the Platonic One, beyond rational articulation, suggests the very ideality and unattainability of such a goal or Focus. The sought-for convergence cannot be shown on the basis of a predictability of history, since the unpredictability of new scientific discoveries spreads to the social and cultural domain. "The new occasions which teach new duties" are thus themselves unpredictable; accordingly, so are the symbolic orderings of future normative as well as factual principles. Worldviews do have axiological aspects. The integrative and organizing functions all subserve worldviews as "interim reports," however and whenever expressed. Yet their overall thrust is toward an ideal but unspecifiable unification.

Difficulties in such anticipations, challenges within older integrations from changing sciences, threats from atavistic nationalisms, and retrogressing religious forces driven by collective egoisms, have all worked to de-stabilize articulated philosophical worldviews. From the 1920s and 1930s, philosophical specialties have prospered, in part because of retreats from "public philosophies" made vulnerable to the strong reactions caused by political promotions—"crusades" of one sort or another, having unforeseen and unlucky side-effects. Philosophers who address a broadly educated public are likely to find their views, and the larger traditions within which they work, subject to attacks which misrepresent their message. The airing of grievances against intelligentsia has been all too easy in an unstable world overstimulated by frenzied campaigns in the media, since public philosophy suggests taking positions and giving reasons for these. The move to "technical" or "professional" philosophy has become most attractive, since the risks in "public" philosophy are so unforeseeable. Philosophy "in the grand manner" has fallen into relative decline. And since Sorokin's forays into philosophy were couched in older styles, these were doubly unwelcome to professionals.

Religious worldviews do not seem in much better shape, where their implementation in modern life has called, so much in vain, for intelligent recognition of social and cultural realities. Obscurantism and the siege mentality, if not that of the jihad, have unfortunately taken hold within a wide range of religious communities. (That is the downside of Sorokin's predictions of an ideational resurgence.) Nonetheless, patient workings toward interfaith understanding here and there persist, lightings of candles rather than cursings of the darkness. In analogy to convergences in philosophy, this quest for some ideal unity bespeaks the hopeful side of perspectivism. Sorokin's integralism and highly catholic and cross-cultural perennial philosophy suggest such a spiritual quest.

There is a special aspect of philosophical non-naturalisms, an aspect shared jointly with religious perspectives. In short, ideational and idealistic expressions share much in common, as Sorokin held. Religions and non-naturalisms are characterized by invocative moments, diversely expressed and grounded, which variously "buttonhole" and draw in their cultural recipients to the acceptance of commended strategies. Religions normally present humankind as addressed by an ultimate reality, thus as having a special status conferred by that very invocation. Philosophies more nearly have persons invoking themselves, as this or that sort of self, and so directing culturated humanity on one or another path.

The witches who hailed Macbeth as Thane of Fife, Thane of Cawdor, and king hereafter, were malign in their intent, nudging their victim in one direction by invoking him in unexpected ways. Religious and philosophical invocations are presumably benign, but no less directive. Consider the range of rationalisms, idealisms and dualisms, phenomenologies (though those are not worldviews, but methodologically perspectival), and existentialisms. Plato invokes the person as soul; Aristotle, as agent intellect (at least at the highest level); Descartes, as *res cogitans*; Kant, as subject and as free noumenal ego; Hegel, as finite *Geist*; Schopenhauer, as *Wille*; Nietzsche, as *Will-zu-macht;* Husserl, as Transcendental Subjectivity; Heidegger, as *Dasein*; and Jaspers, as circumstanced-being, as consciousness-in-general, as *Geist*, and as Existence. All of these hailings counteract more usual and latent self-images, thereby selectively reshaping self-consciousness and either discrediting, demoting, or holding in abeyance other rival modalities of self or culture consciousness. This countervailing activity deploys itself in ways parallel to religious warnings against sin, illusion, or attachment.

As for the promised contrast, systems such as naturalisms, and less systematic approaches, like philosophical analysis, can be alleged to possess invocative features, though these surely operate in a subdued key. Their invocations are more perfunctory and serve no such extraordinary anti-distractive task, even though the naturalist may independently polemicize against idealisms. The naturalist hails persons as inquirers into nature, which they feel themselves to be in any case, just as the analyst hails them as users of language. This is perfunctory because neither is at all surprising, each being a standard and normal mode of awareness. If the witches hailed Macbeth purely and simply as Thane of Fife, he would have taken little notice in view of his knowing himself to be that very noble. We are always taking the "natural point of view" on one hand, and all thought carries with it our basic linguistic enframement on the other. All of this goes without saying; other invocations having their special culturative force, go only with saying. Non-prosaic invocations bring attention to that to which attention is not normally paid.

The role which invocations perform is that of giving extraordinary re-direction to culturative recipients, and sealing off for the time being any other comparable experiential routings from their options. Those, including such sensings and appetites as are activated and aroused in the depths of Plato's Cave, become provisionally devalued as a basis for any total interpretive perspective. Non-naturalisms affirm that special attention has to be paid to cultural projectings and projections, to the salient qualities associated with commended attendings. Among themselves, they differ as to the special inventories of values and priorities suggested therein.

The interest which non-naturalisms, and all secularized sublimations, hold for philosophers of culture derives largely from the shared features of the invocative moment, or the "inward turn." (Such features appear in idealistic and ideational culturations.) That moment stands as a foil to the "outward" turn in objective natural science, technology, and naturalism, all of which are developments of the "natural point of view." Contrary to those, culturative nudgings push us in directions we might not go but for their pressure. The rationalist Descartes set about thrusting moderns into the Enlightenment; Sartre and like-minded phenomenologists worked to push them out of it. Invocations direct and attune humanity to certain susceptibilities, propensities, and vulnerabilities, as opposed to others. Culturative symbolics lends force and gives integrating order to this enterprise.

Nihilism is a factor in a disintegrating, "overripe," demoralized cultural supersystem. At the contrary extreme, any dogmatic exclusivism is tethered locally and inhibits the imaginative movement of *Verstehen* that reaches back in time or outward across cultures. Sorokin's integralism affirms multiple values, and his non-exclusivist "perennial philosophy" is fluid and catholic with the smallest possible "c," drawing as it does on chiefly Western and Eastern traditions of both the ideational and idealistic sorts.

The dogmatist would lock onto automatic pilot and fly full speed into the nearest mountain, while the nihilist would turn off all engines, and nosedive to the ground. The sensible perspectivist believes in keeping aloft by steering, and in continual dialectical improvements for worldviews and other guiding visions. Nihilism could be seen, perhaps over-charitably, as a conclusion drawn from a multiverse of perspectival premises. For Sorokin, nihilism is a pathological symptom of the latest stage of a cultural supersystem, as its inability to rise to the occasion. (For Toynbee, this is the failure to respond to some deadly set of challenges; for Spengler, it is inevitable civilizational decrepitude.) We can look at the rough dialectics of history and see ideational nihilism as religious demoralization such as that brought on by the Black Death (with its *Danse Macabre*), the Hundred Years' War, and clerical corruption-plus-Schism. Idealistic nihilism arises when an aristocratic warrior caste loses it *raison d'être* because of the long bow, say, or heavy artillery. Knighthood no longer flowers. And, most familiar to us, through Sorokin's polemics, worldly urban corruption, a nihilism resulting when thieves fall out. Rough circumstances cut resources for those overly-used to doing well, and competitive strife passes all bounds.

Cultural systems, to which this third of the book addresses itself, reflect such discordant interactions. Cultural change may yet be felicitous, provided it draws upon creative precedents, themselves usually arising from the rough dialectics of past eras. Sorokin likes to allude to such unifying insights as warranted by the Superconscious, each of which implicates some founding Reality.

We have glanced at the dynamics of orientative strategies, including "invocative moments." Invocations imply invokers, and the invoked, selves and transcendent Focal Realities. As selves are commended as having certain proper affinities, that brings value into the picture.

In the next chapter, I will offer a more static structural analysis of Focal Realities, Ideal Structures or values, selves, and the World (as mediation and context for the other sorts).

Seven

CULTURATIVE SYSTEMS: IDEATIONAL AND IDEALISTIC PARALLELS

Now we look at four sorts of factors within philosophical and religious systems, and how these serve as "latching on" places for dialectical blendings among them. The congeniality of idealistic and ideational systems was affirmed by Sorokin, and Randall's accounts of the dialectical origins of religious philosophies in the Hellenistic and medieval periods would seem to provide additional evidence. Nonetheless, the main emphasis here is more on statics than on dialectical dynamics, and in any event mergers are not so much reconfirmations of a once-and-for-all "perennial philsophy" as they are transformations. These are occasionally enriching no doubt, as "felicitous misidentifications," but changes just the same. I remember once that Randall growled, "Aquinas made a hash of Aristotle." (Analogously, F.C. Copleston agreed, but more genially in emphasizing Aquinas's originality and creativity.)

Philosophical theology, building upon overlaps between religion and speculative philosophy, between the ideational and the idealistic, gives stately leads to philosophy of culture. I want to discuss structural analogies and affinities among foundational meaning systems, whether religious or philosophical. Work in philosophy of religion along with metaphilosophical analyses of speculative systems illumines reference points in the history of thought. Too often in recent philosophizings, unsubtle analysts tear claims apart from their contexts. Although this discussion also foreshortens, it points up analogues to clarify normative culturation. Might not these foundational meaning systems be broadly continuous with "myth?"

Sorokin and others have detected parallels in major religions. The most fundamental appears in Ninian Smart's characterization of the "Focus" of religious attention (1973, p. 31) and, likewise in William A. Christian's treatment of the "logical subject" of "basic religious proposals" (1964, pp. 167-209). Pitirim A. Sorokin treats this feature in higher religions (1957, p. 25ff.) as the appropriate object of ideational cultures. Despite differences, other interpretations suggest analogous cultural functions not only in religions but in closely attached philosophies.

We shall discuss the four basic factors. These, together with their inter-relationships, point up similar workings not only in philosophy of religion but also in philosophy of culture. The first constitutes what, modifying Smart's previously mentioned suggestion, I call the "Focal Reality" combining its centrality and high ontological status. It is that about which "basic proposals for belief" are offered. For Judaism and Christianity, this is God; for Islam, Allah; for Hinduism, Brahman; for Confucianism, Tien or Heaven; for southern Buddhism, as both Smart (1973, p. 27) and Christian (1964, p. 20) have maintained, Nirvana; and for Taoism, the Tao.

These comparisons should not be pressed too far, there being no simple common denominators among religions nor among philosophies. Yet some traditions reflect kinship among religious and philosophical "Focal Realities." Philo's enthusiasm was contagious concerning Plato, and this led to developments in theology in which God was identified with Plato's Form of the Good, Plotinus's One, and Aristotle's Unmoved Mover. Again and again speculative philosophers borrow from one another. Hegel not only immanentizes the Plotinian tradition, but he, like Spinoza, takes religion to be a cruder, more metaphorical form of philosophical truth. Spinoza's view is more sophisticated than Stoic pantheism, but his *deus sive natura* bears a strong likeness to the *Logos*.

Descartes and Leibniz each philosophized in light of Christian theology, whether about the Divine Mind or the Uncreated Monad. Though Kant departed from Anselm's and Aquinas's proofs for God's existence, he outlined the moral argument, with its echoes from Protestant and Jewish traditions. Hegel's Absolute Idealism centers upon the notion of infinite spirit, while in recent times Paul Tillich characterized God as "Being-itself" and as the "Ground of Being." In like vein, the philosopher Karl Jaspers refers to the "Transcendent." Many other examples of foundational symbols can be found.

The second factor is the ideal culture, or way of life as differentiated and exalted, for humans to emulate. In the case of Judaism, this is the Divinely revealed Torah; in Christianity, it is Torah as amplified by God's revelation in Christ; in Hinduism, the Vedic laws of Karma; in Buddhism, the sacred teachings or Dharma; in Confucianism, *Li* or sacred tradition; lastly, in Taoism, as in Stoicism, the Focal Reality is seen as continuous with this normative factor. *Tao* signifies "the way to go," as *Logos* does "rationality" or "the way" of nature. For Islam, and other Middle Eastern faiths, the second factor is the revelation of God in his commands, here chiefly those given in the Koran. To summarize, we can say that this aspect is the way of life which finds grounding in Reality.

In the Christian tradition, a duality of revealed and rational moral theology goes far back. In the Epistle to the Romans, Paul alludes to the parallel between the Torah and the Gentile rational moral law. From this, and other reinforcing Greek and biblical elements, developed an account of natural and divine law. This tradition drew upon the Stoic moral cosmos and Platonic Forms for the virtues fitting for human emulation. In Aristotle, the rationalist, teleological, and culminatory component also yield the ideal cultural factor. Plotinus places the Platonic forms in the second Hypostasis. Augustine differs in locating the Divine Ideas in the Mind of God, while modern rationalistic and idealistic philosophers assign innate principles as having rational authority, but less theological relevance. The "clear and distinct ideas" of Descartes, reminiscent of Augustine's illuminism, also the mathematical aspect of reality for Spinoza, both innate ideas and final causes in Leibniz's thought, Kant's synthetic *a priori* categories and categorical imperative, and the Hegelian Ideas, all embody cultural principles claiming acknowledgment, making up the second factor. Such supremely intelligible principles held authority as ways of life and thought, reigning over the exercise of cognitive and moral reason. Recent attacks upon late modernity, as in the realists' "return to reason" movement, show present-day unease with empiricism. Remarkably, Platonism, which so openly affirms the culturative aspect, has shown strong survival powers, defying modernity.

The third factor is the self, subject, or that aspect of the self which is exalted above the world. In and through its invocation, an image of man is established. The image of man is given guidance through the ideal culture, as grounded through the Focal Reality. In Judaism, Islam, and Christianity, man as created by God and called to carry out the Divine will exemplifies this theme. Other instances are the Atman (true self) in Hinduism; the locus of suffering and the starting point for moral effort and release in Buddhism; and humanity, within a generational continuum and destined for immortality, in Confucian thought. Elsewhere, the separation is less sharp. Much as Stoics speak in immanental terms of the soul as "spark of the divine," so Taoists take the self to be continuous with ultimate reality, but in all such cases distinguished from the everyday natural world. Even magical degradations of Taoism confirm this, since the empowered Taoist sage-magician stands apart from the ordinary run of natural events.

Still, the differences between ideational (religious) and idealistic (philosophic) traditions should not be ignored. Philosophers give more weight to autonomous reason, and the history of Western philosophy, unlike that of religious thought, has been entangled with the history of science, reflecting high confidence in theoretical reason. Science and urban values interlock, comfortably or less so, with Greco-European perennial philosophy. The manner in which philosophers differentiate the self from the world typically has exemplified this sanguine attitude.

Additional differences among philosophies can be noted. The Western tradition is indebted to the Platonic intellectualist view of the soul. As a variant upon that, the Aristotelian differentiated self-aspect is *not* his individual life principle that lacks transcendent status, but rather a generic cognizing principle, the "Active Intellect." Another variant in the metaphorical "spark of the divine" is yet another case. With Plotinian thought, individual souls inhabit the domain of the third Hypostasis. For Descartes, the created mind is absolutely pivotal, but Spinoza discusses mental modes devoid of such distinct status. Leibniz treats the soul as a consciously created monad, while the Kantian self is cast in both a rational and a moral dimension as the knowing subject *and* as the "noumenal ego." Hegel takes the self as the finite expression of *Geist*. Even the atheistic existentialist Jean-Paul Sartre, in a reminiscent Cartesian mood, distinguishes the *pour-soi* from the natural *en-soi*.

The self is never just an ordinary component of the natural world for any of these thinkers, but rises to an extraordinary status from the foreground of experience. It is the crucial accession, or "latching-on" point, to experience and thought, and a proximate center for the superorganic. So we could regard religious perspectives as "accession stories," or as sublimated "mythic" accounts of how we find ourselves in a meaningful order, and then take speculative philosophical systems as "accession theories," having a comparable, through more abstract, function. The self, or some aspect thereof, makes contact with a correlative meaningful order. As for more recent thinkers, Ludwig Wittgenstein, in a Kantian vein, once held that the self is not in the world, while existentialists affirm that the subject cannot be objectified.

The fourth factor differentiates itself from the second and third. In the Biblical tradition, it is the created world *other* than humankind. For the Hindu, it is Maya or illusion; for the Buddhist, the order of suffering or bondage; for the Confucian, it is nature, sensitive to disarray from human breaches of the moral order. But for Taoism as for Stoicism, reality is ambiguous, just as the *Logos* is both divine spirit and natural order. There, a comparable ambiguity, one more poetic than speculative, makes it harder to separate the worldly factor in Taoism.

Philosophers, however speculative, try to gear their foundational meaning systems in with the sciences of their age, but the foundings of religious traditions derive from pre-scientific ages. The type of philosophy which deals with the world, unlike differentiated or differentiatable superorganic aspects, draws sympathy from present-day interpreters. It needs no special emphasis here, since we are offering, much in Sorokin's spirit, a culturative counterbalancing of regnant "sensate" interpretations.

Typically, a cleavage opens between the culturative elements and the worldly or "sensate" dimension. The Focal Reality sanctions ways of life and stands as the right object of attention for human beings. As William Christian maintains, the predications of basic religious proposals show both the uniqueness and the primacy of the religious object (1964, pp. 213-217).

What are the relationships and functions of the factors? The first three jointly constitute a supportive and directive setting for cultural "transmissables," to which an "oughtness" attaches. (By a "transmissable" I mean a form of life not merely capable of being transmitted, but one resembling "admissible" evidence in being acceptable or desirable. Higher courts throw out lower court decisions in which "inadmissible" evidence was admitted.) There remains the domain of cognitive symbolics, that is, the intersubjective realm, the common world seen from the "natural point of view," which serves as the stage for human activity. It is prescinded from all subjectivity. It includes matters of empirical factual knowledge and of natural impulse, as does the cave of Plato's myth.

This reading of the two levels, spiritual and natural, or culturative and cognitive, suggests a Durkheim-like identification of the spiritual with the social values of the community, *except* for the way the Focal Reality emphasizes the provisional status of norms and ideals as compared with the eternal Divine itself. Plato's Form of the Good surpasses all other Forms, as in the biblical tradition God's will remains mysterious. Accordingly, we see it would be a mistake to identify society, for example, with the Focal Reality.

"Plato must have read the books of Moses." Here is arguably a "felicitous misidentification." The parallelism between Plato and Judaism, discerned and exaggerated by Philo, led to the Alexandrine Platonizing of Christianity. The different emphasis from purely religious views in Western speculative philosophies lies in their stressing man's cognitive function, conveying a rational way of thought and not the way of life of a community of faith. Philosophers take more notice of science at each stage, and follow a more systematic ideal than do prophets (Christian 1964, p. 233ff.). On the other hand, their views are vulnerable to the effects of scientific and conceptual change.

How do the factors interrelate? First, the Focal Reality provides foundation and authorization for an ideal way of life. It grounds the self, however that may be differentiated, and also the world theater for the active self. The function of normative ways of life, and the subject's provision of an accession point for experience and reality, show us how neither can be a part of the natural world. The superorganic seemingly stands apart. Such foundational systems exclude flat naturalistic accounts of humanity. Though less apparent, this holds true for ambiguous monisms such as Taoism or Stoicism, *and* for the double-aspect monism of Spinoza, given their internalized telic dimension. Otherwise, romantic pantheists, like Goethe, would not be attracted to such views.

Philosophical allusions made until this point have amplified the discussion of religious factors. I now focus that coverage with a summarizing factorial chart. This chart shows the stretching called for to compare all elements; note the differences as seen in Stoicism, Plotinus, and Spinoza. However, the affinities hold the imagination of thinkers, as shown in attempts at so-called or mis-called "perennial philosophy." At the end, I enlisted Sartre to illustrate his opposition to any Focal "in-itself-for-itself"; he too carries traces of a Cartesian dualistic position. The chart has brackets marking departures from the Platonic model, and dots indicating continuities. Continuities for Stoicism and Spinozism are lateral, showing inter-involvement of all factors, unlike those for Plotinus which are unidirectional, marked by arrows. All such continuities contrast with dualistic tendencies in the other thinkers, who sharply divided normatives and subjects from the world.

The status of the world is variable in dualisms and idealisms. As we have seen, it is ambiguous in double-aspect theories and totally regnant in thoroughgoing naturalisms, which this chart cannot represent. One form of naturalism readable as a "counter myth" would be epiphenomenalism, in a curious way a mirror image of Neo-Platonism, where nature had been a by-product of spirit. The chart appears on the next page.

Parenthetically, it has to be noted that charts such as the following constitute garden-variety cases of rational evisagements; they stand as heirs to Plato's "divided line." Key envisagements are reminders of positional contrasts. The present order of the four factors is that of the "Great Chain of Being," while analogues between factors among different positions can serve as "latching-on" places for creative dialectic.

The two charts in this book (pp. 68 and 141) complement the eight included in the Appendix to my *Reanimation in Philosophy* (1986, pp. 175ff.). Those which highlight the culturative functions have particular relevance to my current discussion.

FOUR FACTORS IN SPECULATIVE SYSTEMS

	1. Focal Reality	2. Ideal Structure	3. Self	4. World
Plato	Form of Good	(Other) Forms	soul	*physis*
Aristotle	Unmoved Mover	[essences are <u>in</u> nature]	Active Intellect	*physis*
Stoics	Logos	Structural Aspect	"spark of the divine"	natural side of Logos
Plotinus	First Hypostasis The One ==>	Second Hypostasis *Nous* ==>	Third Hypostasis world-soul ==>	matter, continuous with third
Augustine	God	Divine Ideas	Soul	Created world
Descartes	Divine Mind	"clear and distinct ideas"	created mind	Matter
Spinoza	*deus sive natura*	mathematical order	modes of mind	modes of matter
Leibniz	Uncreated Monad	innate ideas, and final causes	soul, conscious and created monads	Body, Pre-Conscious monads
Kant	God, *Ding-an-sich*	categories, Ideals, categorical imperative	subject, noumenal ego	phenom-enal order
Hegel	*Geist*	Ideas	finite *Geist*	Nature, dependent on spirit
Sartre	[impossible]	[essences are derivative]	*pour-soi*	*en-soi*

Speculative metaphysical theories seem dry as a bone. Yet they, like religious claims, have been labelled by positivism as "emotive." In what senses could they be "emotive?" (Ayer 1948; Lazerowitz 1955). I hold that metaphysics may be emotive in four ways: in unqualifiedly approbative attitudes taken toward the Focal Reality; in imitative approbation toward celebrated ways of life and thought; in self-distinguishing modes of consciousness, each with an emotional tone, whether rationalist or existentialist; or in negative attitudes taken toward unmanageable or threatening aspects of nature, whether as Platonic shadows in the cave, *samsara,* or "absurd" facts giving rise to Sartrean nausea.

The emotional quality of the "belief in" taken towards objects of religious faith or aspiration is clear. In speculative systems, the tone is less intense, but there is the Platonic *eros*, the Spinozist "intellectual love of God," and the satisfaction Aristotle finds in claiming an ultimate principle of intelligibility. Another emotive feature is approbative, in terms of commitment to ways of life or rational principles following from some ultimate reality. The emotional feature attributable to the subjective factor is less obvious, but the tone of self confidence *or* that of forlornness *or* that of rational moral passion remind us of self-delineations. Even more so, religious traditions embody rich modes of self-consciousness, oftentimes negatively with an as yet unresolved human predicament. Finally, the world, taken from a transcendent point of view, may fall under an adverse interpretation. Here too, religious accounts are more emotional than those of philosophy. All such features are more significant than those allowed by logical positivism because of their being geared to systems of interpretations for human experience and its limits.

Philosophers, if not taking speculative views as emotive, often claim that they are "logically odd" or "paradoxical." We may agree when observing departures from common sense realism and science as they focus on transcendent Reality, differentiate the self and ideal culture from the world, and make extraordinary attempts to rejoin that ideal structural order with the world. An example of joining the ideal structural order with the world is Kant's Transcendental Deduction of the categories. But such oddnesses have their point in initiating pursuits of intelligibility and developing accessions to meaning.

Despite differences among major religions, and between those and speculative philosophies, those factors carry analogous sociocultural functions. At a minimum these are directive, supportive, and transformative. The Focal Reality is the key to the differentiation of approbated ways of life and of the self, and sets their basis and limits. The ideal way of life marks directions not given by natural impulse. The differentiated self is the receptor for acculturated experience. In short, humans are not only self-aware as knowers trying to understand their world, but are concerned with sustaining, directing, and transforming culture-consciousness. To put it in Sorokin's terms, they seek integration of values; integralism was his philosophy. Humanity has to cope with limits as well as with creativity, and with the provisionality and the authority of ways of life. For this, humankind may address itself to a religiously or a speculatively conceived One, which centers ways of life and/or thought.

What inferences may be drawn from such dynamic analogies? What weight do they carry? The analysis of accession stories and theories points up degrees of their resemblance and the ways in which they arise from a viewpoint distinct from that of the scientist. In it, culture, though seen as having limits, is authoritative and set over *against* nature. Only through some such account can what Sorokin calls "ideational" and "idealistic" cultures be usefully interpreted. Neither religious views nor speculative philosophies are merely mistaken science, though they are perhaps contingently linked to outdated cosmologies. And that is a most burdensome disadvantage. A different approach should then be taken toward "myth" and similar cultural expressions. In the history of ideas and in many analytical philosophies, too much time is spent apologizing for the supposed ignorance of our ancestors.

I will close with remarks on comparative religion and philosophy. A metacultural theory ought not to be provincial, so here I test the elasticity of its categories by moving toward non-Western faiths and philosophies. This worksheet offers only a scattering of thoughts and reference points for later development. Perennial philosophy, however wide or narrow its construal, and the Biblical Traditions are localized in the West and derive from Athens and Jerusalem. "Philosophical faith" and "religious faith" are more general notions, but are less divided in non-Western cultures, being less shaped by developments in science and political institutions.

While Hinduism melded a mix of nature- and spirit-worship, primitive and social religions, and later attempted its sublimation, Judaism abrogated most such phenomena, or tried to do so. (From one angle, Judaism might be read as a remarkably sublimated national religion.) "Targeting," through Biblical "addressing," and the "inward turn," mystically or rationally expressed, find analogues in the views of Ramanuja on avatars and of Samkara with his non-dualism, respectively.

Diagnostic of the human predicament shows the negative conditions circumstancing the self as a proximate center of meaning, or in other words, as pointing out a gap between proximate and ultimate centers of meaning (for example, the alienation of man from God in the Bible; also *avidya,* through which the self is ignorant of its identity with Brahman). Diagnostic is a prime feature of major religions. One counterpart to diagnostic, strong in the Greco-European Tradition, is the affirmation of human possibilities, which can be taken as positive conditions circumstancing the proximate center, alternatively, as presentation of the affinities between proximate and ultimate centers (such as freedom, creativity, and rationality). World religions typically attest to foundational insights and diagnostics, plus quite extraordinary remedies or salvifics.

Buddhism abandons the intellectually sublimated Hindu tradition. Specifically, it pulls away from its targetings and foundational insights and treats agnostically the proximate and ultimate centers of meaning. One might say that in *lieu* of targeting, it offers diagnostics, or that it targets a provisional center of suffering, and that in *lieu* of foundational insights, it offers the remedy—or its culmination—in Nirvana or the "buddha-nature" (see Smart 1973, p. 67). All this suggests a "withdrawal strategy," *but* the thrust of Western withdrawal strategies is quite different, science-ridden and tending to thoroughgoing scepticism. To the contrary, Buddhism does not totally withdraw from its inherited diagnostic nor from all of the proposed remedies, though dropping traditional Vedic specifics. Something like "addressing" reappears in Mahayana with the Bodhisattvas.

Striking parallels appear in the ways Taoism and Stoicism reflect nature-worship, just as Confucianism and Platonism could be traced to spirit-worship. Yet, those Eastern and Western analogues resist assimilation, the Western Tradition being so preoccupied with science and with a more autonomous political thought.

In summation, non-Western traditions leave less distance between religion and philosophy. "Axial faiths" or "well-founded strategies" integrate clashing ways of life and thought with their moments of targeting, authorizing, and foundational insight. However these are symbolized, they have considerable carry-over, as do their diagnostics and salvifics, even with the qualifications demanded for Buddhist thought. All those—and Greco-European affirmations of human possibility—hark back to their own metaculture. Still and all, analogues must be pursued with some caution, even though key categories are attractive clues to the working of culturative symbolics across all sorts of boundaries. And such crossings of boundaries are demanded by Sorokin's macrosociology.

Eight

WESTERN AND HINDU ROOTS OF PHILOSOPHY

This chapter is a follow-up to "Culturative Systems: Ideational and Idealistic Parallels," gearing in with its comparative factorial analysis. The categorial base is largely drawn from Jaspers and Sorokin.

Naturally, the earlier treatment of Sorokin's insights into Eastern thought provides a clear opening for this discussion. A key point is that Ideational and Idealistic systems in the West hail from different sources (Athens and Jerusalem) and that Indian Ideational and Idealistic systems are genetically related. So only the loosest affinities are to be looked for between Western and Eastern Idealisms. That shows that Sorokin's own "mere variation of the perennial strains of philosophy" cannot be taken as a once-and-for-all doctrine.

My aim is not historic, as would be the case in my showing that common origins form Indo-European language and myth, or that Upanishadic influences upon Greek thought existed; I aim to highlight similar functions, with the aid of metacultural categories. These categories, arising from within Western thought, need wide testing so that the theory becomes less parochial. Section 1 presents the categorial base. Section 2 suggests analogues between Western and Hindu thought. Lastly, Section 3 points out trends dividing the traditions, and placing some strain on the categories.

1. Principles and Categories

The conceptual apparatus, here offered in a Sorokin-influenced metacultural proposal, bridges foundational symbolisms both in religion and philosophy. Three principles will provide an organizing device through which to introduce the categories sequentially.

The maximal metacultural formula, influenced by Karl Jaspers's comments upon the "axial age" and "philosophical faith" (Jaspers 1954, chap. 8), is this: *There are well-founded strategies for autho-*

rizing and integrating ways of life and thought. That is essentially compatible with Sorokin's integralism, and also with John Randall's emphasis on religion's role in unifying values. It covers not only the Biblical Traditions, but also the Greco-European non-naturalisms that I once labelled the Gentile Tradition, and which offer the most prominent analogues for philosophies of the Hindu Tradition. While the Biblical, Western philosophical, and Hindu Traditions are all highly localized notions, at this metaculural level of abstraction they exemplify the structural features of well-founded strategies, or of "axial faiths," slightly modifying Jaspers's term.

Four interrelated features of well-founded strategies give us the categories: first an integrating Focus, or foundational insight to an ultimate source or center of meaning, grounds the strategy; second, authorization for ways of life (including for philosophy, ways of thought) and for the adjustive strategy must exist; third, a targeting of the strategy to its recipient, to the self as proximate focus or center of meaning, occurs: lastly, an accounting for the world, the stage upon which the strategy is played out, has to be set forth.

The Biblical foundational insight, rather more given than achieved, is to a personal God; that of the Greco-European Tradition, rather more achieved than given, leads to a more impersonal Divine. Biblical authorizations come in terms of Divine commands and progressive revelation; Western philosophical authorizations appear in terms of rational acknowledgments and normative self-evidence. Biblical targeting is expressed through special creation and the addressing by God of prototypical forerunners; Greco-European targeting, by a "principle of interiority" or inward turn. Biblically, the world stage has its meaning as the Creation of the Creator; in philosophical terms, as the field of objects "outward" from the proximate focus or knowing subject.

Rootages of these four functions are intimated in common sense. Putting them in reverse order, the "natural point of view," so-called by Husserl, or the practical worldly attitude, is the most noticeable aspect of common sense. The other three are far more latent: self-awareness, the social sense of fittingness, or of approbative emulation, and lastly, the religious sense—a vague awareness of ultimacy. Fully but diversely developed, those four subtly interact to produce axial faiths.

Regarding the origins of Western philosophy, several other categories may be hypothecated. Animism and primitive religion are relatively undistinguished here, and from that fusion or confusion emerge two ideally distinguishable modes: where centers of meaning are treated as separable from nature and where they are treated as embedded in nature. Calling those modes "spirit worship" and "nature worship" oversimplifies the actualities, but offers the convenience of non-Biblical sorts of subterranean trends eventuating in dualistic Platonism and double-aspect monism in Stoicism, respectively. (Aristotelianism, like much else in the Greco-European Tradition, mixes both.)

Having considered the maximal formula, through which obvious comparisons for Hindu philosophy arise, a minimal formula can be devised which allows room for cases in which the Greco-European Tradition is secularized. (Parallel secular interests within Hindu thought seem served by differentiation within a tradition nominally addressing problems of liberation or *moksha* [Potter 1972, chap. 1 and *passim*].) My recommended minimal formula is: *It is necessary to place humanity jointly within a normative culture and the world.* While integrating culturation and world description are reasonably covered by the maximal formula (where the integrating Focus is central), secularized versions do not feature the Focus or foundational insight. De-numinized dualist and mixed residues, with other ineradicable traces of the allegedly Perennial Tradition, survive only to be carped at by reductionist analysts like Ryle, Quine, and Rorty.

The third formula, or following dictum, belongs not to metaculture but to analytic metaphilosophy: *It is necessary for philosophy that ways of life, thought, and talk be analyzed and clarified.* C. D. Broad on "Critical Philosophy" (Broad 1953, p. 82f.), John Austin on the linguistic "begin-all" (Urmson 1967, p. 236), John Passmore's rejection of the mere sage (Passmore 1967, p. 217ff.), all express this dictum. The analysis of common sense, experiential, conceptual, or linguistic, and that of science, together with methodological prescriptions for inquiry, may, but need not necessarily, lead to antimetaphysical withdrawal strategies seeking the dis-integration of well-founded strategies and placements alike. The dictum in its innocuous form is universally accepted, as it does not confine philosophy to analysis. "Clarity is not enough" (Lewis 1963). Still, echoes of current Western dis-integrative preoccupations are detectible in anti-Vedantist scholars of Indian philosophy. (For example, Matilal's *Journal of Indian Thought* [1971] was open to non-Vedantist positions.)

2. Analogues

How far one can go with the following comparisons is an open question. But for the time being, my project is to seize upon and make much of any analogues in sight.

Samsara, a necessary element in the Hindu diagnostic of man's predicament, can be read as a curious blending of spirit-and nature worship. Both separability from, and embeddedness in, nature seem affirmed as centers of meaning, considering both transfer at death and interim localizations. (By contrast, we can say that Plato himself was not quite so serious about transmigration, given the Greek culture, but that he gave the notion a "mythic" or poetic deployment.)

Regarding Western and Hindu scriptures, a remarkable contrast in defensive apologetics throws light on Greco-European and Hindu authorizing tactics. The eternality asserted for the Vedas suggests the supratemporal status given Plato's Forms, rather than the historically revelatory Biblical mode. But as in Biblicism, this serves to protect the scriptures against historical criticism.

As to philosophies, we turn first to heterodox views. Cãrvãka parallels Western naturalisms—and such naturalisms have in common the basing of culturation solely upon natural worldly descriptions—as well as skeptical withdrawal strategies. Worldly "outwardness" is primary, other intimations being dismissed. On the other hand, Buddhist thought deploys withdrawal strategy in an anti-speculative, yet not anti-religious way, pulling back from certain conventional salvifics and from Upanishadic speculation. Anatta was compared quite subtly with the Humean self by Ambassador Malalasekra in a lecture I heard at Northwestern University in 1954; but still, those skepticisms work to different ends. Rather than any simple targeting of a metaphysical self, there is an overriding diagnostic of the center of suffering. In place of foundational insight, one might still say there is an integrating Focus merged with the Buddhist salvific (Smart 1973, p. 67).

Among Orthodox Hindu schools, Sãmkhya (and possibly Vedantist Dvaita) suggests Western dualisms among foundationalist non-naturalisms. To follow critical observations made by Professor Organ, the nonpolar character of Sãmkhya may make it hard to go too far with that (Organ 1976, pp. 33-39). Yoga, more strongly than Sãmkhya, emphasizes the inward turn in its practical preoccupation.

Schools within Vedanta yield still more comparisons. Advaita emphatically suggests Western absolute idealism, viewed here as a limiting case of double-aspect monism where the worldly aspect attenuates to a near vanishing point. As *Natur* is a function of *Geist*, so Maya is of Brahman. (The illusionist aspect of Maya seems more pronounced than that of its Western counterpart.)

On the other hand, Ramanuja's qualified non-dualism matches a more balanced double-aspect monism. Incidentally, discussions of Nirguna and Saguna Brahman recall the *via negativa* and *via affirmativa*. A contrast is that Ramanuja's well-founded strategy can be targeted through Vishnuite addressing, Samkara's being limited to the inward turn.

Tantrism and Sri Ramakrishna show more popular religious aspects, though the sympathetic reading Zimmer gave them, along with Organ's advocacy of polar dualisms (Organ 1976, p. 35), encourage our allowing Tantrism as a complex analogue to double-aspect monism. As far as updated Vedantism is concerned, Professor Radhakrishnan's downplaying of Advaitin illusionism offers a frame for sublimated Hinduism capable of exchanges with the Greco-European.

Nyaya and Vaisesika can be interpreted either in relation to moksha, as by Professor Potter (1972, chap. 1), or in terms of the more stringent version of the analytic dictum; one difference is that in Indian thought logic fuses with epistemology (Matilal 1971).

3. Differentiations

Historically, the Hindu Tradition carried more from the past and had more to sublimate than did the West. The gap between Jerusalem and Athens, as well as monotheist zeal, affected their later representatives, accentuating housecleaning impulses from theology and philosophy, thus paring back primitive traces of the sort India retained.

Western and Hindu Traditions consequently deal differently with social customs and actual habits of adaptation, ways of life, and ways of doing. Hinduism takes a more sublimatory stance and Westerners essay a more confrontational mode, Biblically prophetic or philosophically critical. Hinduism conglomerated and gently adjusted its heritage; biblicists and Greco-European philosophers abrogated and vigorously reworked theirs when they saw fit. (Yet, Hindu "*re*valorization," to put Eliade's term in the service of Jaspers's view of the Axial Age, cannot be underestimated either [Eliade 1978, pp. 230ff.].)

Obviously, Hindu philosophy, unlike the Greco-European perennial tradition, has an organic relation with its religious tradition through its diagnostic and salvific, while the Biblical and Greco-European Traditions coexisted in mutual aggravation but occasional profit. Of course, Indians do pursue specialized interests within that frame. Still, diagnostic and salvific are farther from the presuppositional frame of the Western perennial tradition, and that may lead to misreadings even by sympathetic Indians. Keeping in mind prudent admonitions against global accountings, each still have preponderancies which differ. Religious faith and "philosophical faith" are distinguishable at least in the West.

Lastly, the pursuit of self-awareness is by no means the same (Scharfstein 1978, p. 205ff.; see also Zimmer 1969, pp. 409ff.). Both the Western perennial and Hindu traditions turned inward, but for the West this turn was an attempt at making the true self; for the Hindu tradition this turn was an un-making of an illusory self. (In the Biblical Tradition, different still, a Divine addressing, its proper mode of targeting, intends the re-making of a mis-made self.)

While changes in the philosophical atmosphere, from the Golden Age to linguistic analysis, from Radhakrishnan to Matilal, make piecemeal exchanges on the level of the analytic dictum far easier than on the level of metacultural theory, broad civilizational concerns call for a more old-fashioned, if difficult, inquiry. Sorokin's rough dialectic in his *Dynamics* especially forces the issue.

Nine

SOROKIN'S CULTURAL THEORY AND WESTERN THOUGHT

An early version of this discussion was read to the regional meeting of the Society of Christian Philosophers at Virginia Commonwealth University in Richmond, and it was published in an earlier form in Explorations.

One can say that typological statics and historical dynamics are here combined, as are the Randallian and Sorokinian dialectics for philosophy. (The same applies to "Sorokin and Cross-Cultural Comparisons," which offers the natural context into which this approach fits.)

Pitirim A. Sorokin set forth a broad view of cultural oscillations, depicting severe civilizational crises provoking swings from religious ("ideational") eras toward secular ("sensate") ones, and vice versa, sometimes with an intermediate ("idealistic") transition following the ideational. The following citations express his triadic culturology:

> Besides these vast cultural systems [religion, language, fine arts, law and ethics, politics and economics,] there are still vaster cultural unities that can be called cultural supersystems. As in other cultural systems, the ideology of each . . . is based upon . . . certain ultimate principles. . . . The vastest of these are the supersystems whose major premises or ultimate principles concern the nature of the ultimate true reality or the ultimate true value. Three main consistent answers have been given. One is: "The true, ultimate reality-value is sensory. Beyond it there is no other reality or any other nonsensory value." This premise and the gigantic supersystem built upon it is called the *sensate* supersystem.
>
> Another answer . . . is: "The true, ultimate reality-value is a supersensory and superrational God (Brahma, Tao, Divine Nothing, and other equivalents of God)." . . . This premise and its corresponding

> cultural supersystem is called *ideational.*
>
> The third answer to the question is: "The true, ultimate reality-value is the Manifold infinity, which contains all differentiations and which is infinite qualitatively and quantitatively. The finite human mind cannot grasp it or define it or describe it adequately in its infinite plenitude. . . . Only by a very remote approximation can we discern three main aspects in it: the rational or logical, the sensory, and the superrational-supersensory. . . .
>
> This typically three-dimensional conception of the ultimate and the supersystem built upon it is described as *idealistic or integral.*
>
> Each of these three supersystems embraces in itself the corresponding type of the vast systems already described . . . . (Sorokin 1966, pp. 23-24)

Though Sorokin sometimes oversimplified the application of his account to the history of philosophy, paying special attention to our "sensate" crisis and, so, to possibilities for religious renewal, provides a provocative topic. In the following I attend to features of ideational, idealistic, and sensate cultures that seem the most salient, give a Neo-Sorokinian tracing of Western philosophy, and close with addenda to Sorokin's diagnosis of the "overripe sensate" age.

1. Salient Features of the Cultural Types

What events are most representative of ideational perspectives? Exemplifications of roles or patterns of life taken as grounded in sacred reality, divinely warranted acts of virtue (saintly ones, for instance)–these counterpoised by those translucent to the divine, but mediating darkness or the demonic–are such events. ("The Devil made me do it," said Geraldine.) Also to be included are ritual actions, recapitulative of revelatory or miraculous events central to a faith. Providential happenings or their cross-cultural equivalents provide keys to theologies, or brahmologies or buddhologies, of sacred history. Behind the patterns stand larger integrations of meaning, and these shine through.

Idealistic culture is continuous with ideational, yet shifts toward ideal patterns worthy of respect and emulation for their own sake may ensue. Such virtues are celebrated in ideal leadership roles, both rational and practical. Consequentialism does not yet enter the picture; sages like Socrates and Spinoza and knights and princes of great virtue show forth intrinsically worthy forms of life. That these figures are "idealized," rather than portrayed "warts and all," has profound significance.

The arts, especially literature, contain moral touchstones, expressive of types celebrated in the dominant culture. Contrast the Knight of the *Canterbury Tales* with the bourgeoisie, or the Parson and the Nun's Priest with the opportunistic church figures. Also briefly mentioned by Chaucer was the ideal humble peasant, the Plowman. (The medieval list of basic functions being "To fight, to pray, to work.") Ideational culture takes events and roles as reflecting the Divine, positively or negatively. Idealistic culture shifts attention more to the worthy pattern and social role itself, warranted by the greater scheme of things, *but* commendable in its own terms as well.

With sensate culture, practical actions seen as goal-related and geared to sensual payoffs, along with sensory observations as clues to further observations, become more salient. Patterns here lose their inherent value, whether rational or normative; instrumentalism takes over. "Maturity" of the sensate stage, we shall see, still must be differentiated from its overripeness, where maladaptations herald sensory clues and cues undercutting needed forms of life. With the sensate at its best, mindlessness by no means yet reigns. Sorokin showed a sense of balance in his preference for "integralism," where neither otherworldly nor worldly cultural style monopolized.

2. The Western Tradition as Undergirded

Sorokin's treatment of the history of philosophy is broad and rather neglectful of the trends upon which post-Enlightenment European thinkers concentrate. Nevertheless, Sorokin's view of civilizational crises and their results gives a harsh, much-needed qualification for liberal progressivism. Understandably, Westerners did not fully appreciate Sorokin's *Social and Cultural Dynamics*. Sorokin's background in Russia, where there was no Renaissance and little Enlightenment, together with his drastic disillusionments with progressivism, account for the cultural gap between himself and American contemporaries. He is best on the "ideational" and "idealistic" cultures, less fair to the "sensate." He takes a longer view of "rhythms" or "oscillations" than structural-functionalists and pragmatists ever could. This longer view stressed the rough dialectic of crises and calamities which undermine value systems.

No definite periodicity was implied by "rhythm," nor did Sorokin affirm any absolute pure type. He qualified his position casually in passing, while his critics stodgily worked from the limited basis of his most conspicuous rhetoric. But even as qualified, his often polemical treatment of philosophy still requires adjustments.

The theory of Sorokin can be brought into sharper focus. Underlying the three phase oscillation is the integral human situation with four basic aspects. One of these, practical outwardness, comports well with the sensate phase. The factor authorizing norms by means of emulation coordinates with structural and axiological themes in his idealistic supersystem. Lastly, a transcendent religious insight alludes to the Reality which Sorokin takes as ideational. The mystical turn inward to the subject serves as the point and pivot of creativity for both idealistic and ideational cultures. Inwardness correlates with outwardness, invoking the point of renewal, where creative *re*-viewing occurs in movements toward or within ideational and idealistic cultures.

The human situation calls for practical adaptation to the world, through qualitative immediacies as clues to the future and as cues for action. Humankind necessarily begins within such sensory presentations. Next, humanity's social nature calls for acknowledging and following role models. Upon this, idealistic culture rises with its encouragement of needed patterns, conveyed both to those who should follow them and those who should defer to them. Lastly, the shocks of human history, let alone personal crises, demand reintegration of norms clashing with one another and with circumstances. This clash summons an ideational grounding for their renewed authority within its reconciling symbolic matrix. Sorokin calls our attention to the synthesizing status of the idealistic between ideational and sensate, by showing religious insights in the background of idealistic culture.

In the long view, not only progressive trends, but also rhythms may be discerned. How does one make sense of rhythms? We may ask what mechanisms of change cause always-present factors to be highlighted at various stages. An idealist era grows from an ideational one as that order becomes locally imposed and aristocratic commendations of role models become socially desirable. When power long since had decentralized itself, making rewards uncertain, persuasion and idealized virtue become crucial, to coax emulation from the creative minority and demand deference from the supportive majority. Ideal philosopher-guardians and warriors, learned clergy and knights, draw on patterns worthy of emulation. Seemingly, idealistic culture grounds itself on greater wealth and order than could an ideational one, even though the reward pattern has not become capable of bourgeois rationalization as analyzed by Max Weber.

For the ideational era, God, or some other Focus, must be center stage. Ninian Smart uses the term "Focus" to allude to the object of worship (1973, pp. 62ff.). Idealistic culture shifts from that Focus toward commended ways of life. The rational principles to be acknowledged by the true philosopher are illustrative.

In the next shift, the overriding emphasis departs *both* from the Divine and Idealized Human, and attends to sensory immediacies as clues to the world and cues for appetition. Thus, cultural thematics move from the idealistic to the sensate. Prosperous causal conditions for this phase include centralization of secular authority, as with rising national states, a more ordered market place, heightened social mobility and meritocracy, not to mention a felt need, diffused within the economy but concentrated within the government, for fine-tuning behaviors of subjects, citizens, and producer-consumers by "rationalizing" rewards and punishments. Thereby, a range of economic and political motives, reinforced by technocracy engaged with science, highlight the immediate and empirical. Thinkers from Hobbes, through Bentham and Mill, to Weber and Drucker, make that point.

However, vulnerable sensate values stand on institutions not solid for all times. In the course of human affairs Fortune's wheel spins wildly. Relative transfers of advantage add up to substantial trends. When great enough in degree and number, they undermine the weightiest social structures, demoralizing elites and populace alike, both already weakened by overstimulated expectations. Those elites themselves may collapse and frequently do. The operative motto becomes "*après moi le déluge,*" or more typically in our age, "take the money and run." (As with those responsible for our four trillion dollar debt.) In the "overripe" stages of sensate cultures, orgies or jet-setting for the elites, and bread and circuses–or food-stamps and moon shots–for the populace are made available.

We can now scan the Western philosophical tradition in relation to its social background. The idealist culture roughly matches (though sometimes lagging behind) aristocracy, the privileged group within which traditions of excellent life and service became internalized. Those outside the aristocracy were trained, or coerced, into deference. No doubt the aristocratic ideal invariably finds only imperfect and unstable expression. The admitted precariousness of Sorokin's idealist supersystem surely supports that conclusion.

Three of the four Athenian schools, Platonism, Aristotelianism, and Stoicism, differ from Epicureanism in their idealist orientation. Plato had resisted Homeric transmutations of ideational myth, as well as sensate Sophism. The Stoics founded a tradition bound to appeal to Roman gentry. An aristocratic ethos had characterized Aristotle who, while continuing Platonic themes, also shaped his philosophy into a broad supportive matrix for science. In metaphysics, rational psychology, ethics, and politics, classical and post-classical Athens left examples of what would exemplify idealist thought for Sorokin. The late Hellenistic collapse generated a major shift in sociocultural style.

After that change, St. Augustine, living amidst utter crisis, produced mainly ideational work with idealist buttressing. Later in the more stable high Middle Ages, Aquinas attended to the natural world, thus becoming more "integral" in Sorokin's sense. Subsequently, Descartes's "inward-outward" epistemological and metaphysical dualism opened the door for mechanism, while leaving ideational and rationalist elements central to his thought.

John Locke moved closer to the sensate spirit with his empiricism, while still mixing a rationalist approach to ethics and the law with an innovative sensate epistemology. In all major respects, David Hume and later utilitarians offered a far more mature sensate position. Immanuel Kant, unfortunately underrated by Sorokin, fused sensate and idealist elements far more subtly than could his predecessor Locke. Kant's astute awareness as to what science evolved into and what the inherited idealist approach has to give science, constitute lasting contributions.

Goethe and Rousseau, as well as post-Kantians from Fichte to Hegel, could be variously taken. Under the rubric of Romanticism, theirs were mature sensate expressions on the subjective side of feeling and volition, not on the objective sensate side of perception. Also, they were idealists, not in Sorokin's special sense, but through their subjectifying and internalizing of religion. In contrast, naturalists, whether realists or phenomenalists, took mature sensate positions in the cognitive, not in the affectively romantic, style. Recently, John Dewey's instrumentalism, unlike Bentham's Utilitarianism, had absorbed the lesson of the Darwinian revolution.

Currently, just as in the late nineteenth century, "overripe sensate" culture shows itself through scientific and romantic nihilisms. Scientific nihilism descended from the mature sensate on the cognitive side; romantic nihilism manifested the sensate in its volitional and affective aspect. Logical positivism and skeptical philosophical analysis, each withdrawing from any classical ties with traditional norms and sublimated mythic elements, sometimes tend toward scientific nihilism. In contrast, Nietzsche, Sartre, and Heidegger, for example, embody the overripe sentimental sort.

The dominant cultural ambiance does not exclude the coexistence of alternative philosophical types. While the regnant "supersystemic" style does not mark philosophy in all details, it does heighten the audibility of views matching the reigning mode through rewards, encouragements, and discouragements. Of course, no complete cultural homogeneity could ever be reached, even in principle.

What about the mechanisms of modernity which accentuate sensate themes within our own tradition? Roughly from the Renaissance and the rise of the national state, we see how increasingly centralized rewards and punishments have worked. Consider Henry Tudor bestowing monastery lands upon his backers, and using the Star Chamber for his enemies. Later in the same English territory, Thomas Hobbes preached a prudential obedience owed to any sovereign whosoever in full possession of powers adequate to reward or punish.

Subsequently, Adam Smith expounded on the benign "hidden hand" of the economic marketplace, a more far-reaching reward system than any boasted by a secular ruler. On the political side, Bentham instructed the "many-headed" Legislator in how to administer the state by distributing pleasure and pain. The founder of Utilitarianism had mathematicized the common good into the greatest happiness of the greatest number. Recently, on our side of the Atlantic, a celebrated behaviorist has kindly tried to extricate us from idealist "freedom and dignity" (Skinner 1972). The underlying sociopolitical assumptions stayed the same in all such cases, while secularists, now as then, vigorously seek release from idealist remnants like natural law and natural rights. The preceding history sets the scene for a few observations upon what presently stimulates our "overripe" sensate culture.

3. "Overripeness" Leading to Nihilism

Romanticism had begun to turn sour as early as Schopenhauer and Nietzsche. To the extent that Romanticism defensively retreats back into the self, driven by acute disillusion with the pressures of society and the world, romantic nihilism takes hold. The further the Romantic fled from rational affirmation of moral and natural order, the less chance remained for any cultural balance. Many late Romantics accordingly became "roll-your-own" mythmakers, departing from the Perennial tradition to nurture peculiar visions of their own.

Accordingly, the late nineteenth century made room for nihilism in politics. That of Bakunin's cohorts forced open the door for Marxist autocracy in Russia. The Sartrean nihilism assisted splendidly in giving Marxist thought temporary respectability in France. Further, we should consider the political timing of Heidegger's passively romantic nihilism. Heidegger dolefully deplored what he called the "forgetfulness of Being," this being his personal rationale for jettisoning the classical tradition with all its close involvements with scientific and moral reason. What remains can be labelled an aesthetico-mystical residue of ontology, and its use by post-Heideggerian litterateurs befits the anomic state of modernist art. Though personality had been painted in more worldly colors, it had remained intact in mature sensate literature. In late modernism, it is either totally swamped or dissolved.

On political and economic fronts, discontents with rotting secularity have led to conditions favoring ideational renewals. Khrushchev's secret 1956 speech and revelations by others about the Gulag, not to mention failures of economic leadership, all undermined Russian Communist zeal. In 1989 total collapse followed. At the opposite ideological pole, "put not your faith in presidents" might well become the motto for Americans. Once enthralled by the victories of the Second World War, we have been treated in succession to a Korean stalemate, a Bay of Pigs, a Vietnamese defeat, runaway inflation, the resignations of a vice-president and a president in disgrace, an Iranian fiasco (with its own ideational aspects), the tripling of the national debt in two presidential terms, and NATO dabblings in the Balkans. Parallel to these events arrived unfavorable trade balances of unprecedented scope. Neither political party has been able to do more than palliate the consequences, or to kite checks through tax-cut promises.

Religious stirrings are visible, in reinvigorated Catholicism in Europe, and in religiously inspired nationalist revolts all around the fringes of Western empires. Though qualitative discriminations must be made concerning all such responses, what is clear is that trust in secular institutions has been eroding, along with the moral tone in the arts, media, and public life.

4. Closing Observations

Three propositions help give order to the preceding explorations.

Evidence supports all three; and all open broad questions in philosophy of culture and civilization.

Proposition 1: "Ideational" cultural forms, roughly in Sorokin's sense, perennially reappear. Nowadays they display surprising liveliness, sometimes to the point of intrusiveness: expressions of dissent and violent reaction have been taking religious form. A few of these modes, unhappily "pseudo-ideational" rather than authentic, mix reactionary content with up-to-date communications and terrorist techniques. All this lends assured credibility to Sorokin's theory of supersystemic oscillation. Incidentally, it proves the need for sociology and history of religions, especially in hopes of stimulating positive ideational creativity.

Proposition 2: A strong affinity and continuity holds between ideational and idealistic cultural elements. Sorokin affirms this through his integralism and in detailed recountings of historic trends. In their time, Mohandas Gandhi and Martin Luther King, Jr., each illustrated joint appeals to broadly idealistic traditions of law *and* to ideational groundings for those. In keeping with this ideational/idealistic continuity, strong connections obtain between religion, philosophy, and politics.

Proposition 3: Ideology has emerged as a danger in our "overripe" crisis, carrying the threat of secular fanaticism as a counterpart to anti-ideational and anti-idealistic nihilisms. This normative disease pretends to scientific objectivity, but only to sanctify favored roles for favored groups. The mirror opposites of Neo-Manchesterian and Marxist ideologies, whose messages boil down to "All power to the oligarchs (or party bureaucrats)!", share the fallacy of forgetting the sociocultural dimension in pursuit of abstract models of political economy. This neglect constitutes a special ingredient of our "overripe sensate" culture, feeding into bloodier forms of dissent and reaction. Speaking of ideology, Freudianism, in its popular and commercial expressions, could be metaphorically construed as a self-regarding ideology for private life, while Marx and Manchester between them professedly divide the whole public realm.

Concluding Moral: Philosophies of all sorts, together with varied approaches to religious and civilization studies, could most profitably be taken as *showing the possibilities and the dangers of culturative symbolics*, that is, of worldviews whether religious, philosophical, or ideological. That joint task may be our most relevant pursuit of wisdom, the deepest "critique of institutions" available to scholars today. Materials from the histories of philosophy and religion together with Sorokin's thought, used as a key interpretive method, establish a beginning for that pursuit. Worldviews and guiding visions give us different orientative strategies, while perspectivism is their matrix.

Ten

SOROKIN AND CROSS-CULTURAL COMPARISONS

This chapter combines statics and dynamics, that is, structural functional analysis of philosophical and religious systems with historical dialectics, both progressive and rough.

The influence of Randall overlaps with that of Sorokin, as it does in Chapter Nine, "Sorokin's Cultural Theory and Western Thought," where Western specifics are spelled out in detail. The larger contexts for looking at exceptional phenomena, especially from Eastern cultures, are here sketched in, animating typological clues for cross-cultural comparisons. Section 1 lays the groundwork, and section 2 amplifies the Neo-Sorokinian strategy.

Just as this chapter follows up on the earlier discussion of perspectivism, so it anticipates further examination of Sorokin's integralism as a "mere variation of perennial strains in philosophy" (Allen 1963, p. 373).

1. Setting the Contexts for Civilizational and Intellectual Phases

Civilizational responses to crises of adversity, of painfully acquired social order, of growing prosperity, and of the gluttony and folly that toss society back into adversity, include selective heightening or diminution of the audibility of certain philosophies. Occasions for such responses cross civilizational bounds, mediated through internal and external social environments. A civilization's dissidents sort polemical values from neighboring cultures in a revisionary way. Though technical culture travels with less change, ideal culture ripped from its context can move swiftly enough. Drastic upheavals take on cultural forms, making for dramatic intellectual history, and Sorokin's rough dialectic encompassed a range of such dramas.

Consequently, one good way to apply sociology to intellectual history would be to compare leading types of philosophy through their changing phases in terms of a slightly revised Sorokinian interpretation. Apparent difficulties arise: the co-presence of contrasting philosophies; more generally, man's perpetual involvement with faith, ideal role models, and sensory experience; and the refusal of Eastern cultures to show the same fluctuations as the West. Yet, none of these will turn out to be crucial objections to this approach. Sorokin was far more cautious in laying out his theory than his rhetorical flourishes sometimes suggested to his critics.

Sorokin did not claim that the oscillations found in Western civilization had to be replicated elsewhere. "I nowhere claimed that such an order of succession is a universal uniformity" (Sorokin 1941, p. 770). Some other order could be possible, or even a rhythm in which the sensate stage was not attained. "Some cultures never reach an integrated level from this (idealistic) standpoint, while some others like, for instance, the Brahmanic culture of India, have remained in the ideational phase far longer that either the Greco-Roman or the Western culture" (Sorokin 1941, p. 771).

Nonetheless, Sorokin responded to criticism that less complete rhythms are found in Brahmanic culture. "On the other hand, in my concise statements regarding the Hindu-Brahmanic culture (not the whole culture of India, but only its Brahmanic or Hinduist aspect) I indicated time and again that even it has known periods of an increase and a decrease of its influence upon the whole culture of India" (p. 771, note 45). Again, he writes: "Likewise, a somewhat similar, though not as pronounced, rhythm has been pointed out as happening several times in other cultures—the Egyptian, the Hindu, the Chinese" (p. 425).

In light of Sorokin's position, why should a neo-Sorokinian approach be pursued? As suggested earlier, Sorokin stood alone in his defiance of the main trends in Western sociology. His countervailing insights, bringing his long-run approach to bear against short-run complacencies, have much to offer to history of philosophy. Parallels are found in the approach taken by F. C. Copleston, who offers positive readings of ideational and idealistic thinkers, but some creative tension ensues between Sorokin and John Herman Randall, Jr. Randall is sympathetic in presenting the gradual maturing of Western sensate culture, while showing sensitivity to idealist remnants; but his general approach is arguably unidirectional, following the sequence of dialectical scientific challenges to older values.

Sorokin, by contrast, was tone-deaf to the Western European tradition. His own personal history of disillusionment with Western progressivism overlay a deep Russian background. Russia had experienced neither a Renaissance nor Reformation, and only a drastically foreshortened, even localized, Enlightenment. The mediation of Western values and science achieved by Kant and his successors, including our Cambridge pragmatists, made little impact on the strong-minded Sorokin. What the West ignored out of wishful thinking called for salutary reminders, yet the strenuous terms in which Sorokin's reminders were couched call for qualification, with more acceptance for voluntarism and nominalism, in short for individual action.

From a broader perspective, Sorokin *and* a few sensible critics share some common ground. For example, American pragmatism, Harvard theory of social action, and Sorokin's culturology jointly stake out a way to make sense of causes and reasons in human affairs. Furthermore, the strained duality between absolutism and a relativized historicism, or between ontology and phenomenology, need not prevail. External causes set the scene, human agents confronting precedents in action that commend themselves either as effective (the sensate emphasis), or as normative fulfillments of meaningful human roles (the idealistic emphasis), or as supra-human actions commending both a ritual recapitulation and conformings to Divinely warranted norms (the ideational emphasis). Clearly, pragmatism and structural-functionalism make better sense of particular effective actions, and Sorokin of the normative and supra-human actions. Agents, once causes have unsettled their norms and expectations, must look again for new patterns of reasons, drawn as "forms of life" from instances, comparable to a range of noticed alternatives and imagined possibilities. This range must be limited, life being so short.

Secondly, the Americo-Sorokinian matrix could generate a more plausible aid to political philosophy than any of our technocratic ideologies, Neo-Manchesterian or Marxist. Sorokin, on the idealistic and ideational side, adds depth and range, despite himself, to the American account of action, given in a mature sensate form but structured by inherited Kantian norms.

By noting prevailing cultural controls and the mechanisms which shift reigning cultural supersystems, we may throw light not only on Western trends but also on how and why Hindu and Chinese philosophies have had less pronounced swings between extremes. I shall discuss the ways Western philosophy measures up to Sorokin's "oscillations"; then more briefly, the way Eastern thought fails to do so; and finally, offer proposals on the mechanisms of cultural control and change.

As for influences explaining transitions matching up with Western civilization, from ideational to idealistic, from idealistic to sensate, and from sensate under dissolution to ideational again, Sorokin does not spell out a complete explanation. His principles of immanent change, of limits, and of the relative inadequacy of extreme ideational and sensate beliefs do little more than frame the problem. Still he does not ignore causal forces. As the comments F. R. Cowell gleans from Sorokin on economics show us, non-ideal conditions nurture or inhibit some sociocultural systems (1970, p. 208). Once these insights are placed in the service of long-term institutional trends, where political likelihoods become measured, a more rounded explanation becomes available, just as Sorokin's ideal emphasis becomes reduced. Philosophical developments correlate with such changes.

What sociocultural mechanisms cause the aspects to be differently highlighted over time? An Idealist era follows from an Ideational one to the extent that typically aristocratic commendations of, and appeals to, key role models, become more desirable. When power decentralizes, making rewards uncertain, persuasion and idealization come to the fore, coaxing emulation from the minority and extorting deference from the majority. Ideal philosopher-guardians and warriors, Brahmins and Kshatriyas, and learned clergy and knights must draw upon aristocratic emulation. Presumably, Idealistic culture calls upon greater wealth and order than does the Ideational type, the latter centering as it does upon the Divine reality needed to authorize and integrate those social values suffering from drastic crisis.

In an ideational era, God or some comparable Focus must be central. But in the (possible) successor age of Sorokin's idealism, a *relative* shift takes place toward commended ways of life or idealized roles and their content, for instance, those rational principles to be acknowledged by the true philosopher. In the third great phase, our main attention leaves both the Divine and Idealized Humanity for sensory immediacies as clues to the world and cues for appetition. Conditions for this era include centralization of secular authority, an ordered marketplace, heightened social mobility, and a consequent felt need for fine-tuning all the behavior patterns of subjects, citizens, and producer-consumers. In that manner, simple economic and political motives, reinforced by their scientific ally, bring the immediate and empirical front and center.

By the way, a dominant cultural control system does not exclude the coexistence of different philosophical types. The reality is that a range of views always survives, though not all prosper equally under the cultural pressures.

I turn now to Sorokin on Eastern traditions. Oscillations are less pronounced in the Chinese tradition and much less so in the Hindu, according to Sorokin (Sorokin 1937, vol. 1, chap. 3). Within Hindu philosophy, only the minor school of Carvaka could be labeled sensate. The six orthodox schools have to be taken as ideational, or as idealistic, since, of these, Samkhya counts for Sorokin as the most sensate, though "it is but rationalistic idealism" (Sorokin 1937, vol. 2, p. 58). Brahmanism, Buddhism, and Jainism all strike Sorokin as ideational, as does Taoism within the Chinese tradition. The constancy of the Hindu ideational emphasis, with the reign of the Brahmin decentralized theocracy over two thousand years, means that their philosophy and art could not veer in a strongly sensate direction. It is arguable that the more recent sensate elements should be attributed to Western imports. Some Hindu sensate elements do show up of course; Kautalya's political philosophy, like that of the legal realist Yang Choo, matches with the "cynical sensate" *Il Principe* of Machiavelli, but such themes in Hinduism are minor ones overall.

China differs in that Ideational Taoism and the imported but locally transformed Buddhism contrast more sharply with the "Mixed" or "Idealistic" position of Confucianism. Oscillations in Chinese philosophy and art, with a rather sensate trend cresting under the middle T'ang dynasty, are far more clear than in India's (Cowell 1972, pp. 59f.). Still, even these do not completely match the much stronger Western swings toward sensate values.

Sorokin refused to be bound to any notion that the supersystemic three-phase pattern *has* to be universal across civilizations, though the point may not be widely recognized by his critics. That concession, once made, does not vitiate the value of his position, since the ideational, idealistic, and sensate labels have meaning for sorting philosophies and other cultural products. To reconcile constant sociocultural factors with civilizational variations across the temporal vector, we should test suppositions like the following:

> As every unhappy family is unhappy in its own way, so different civilizations meet their periods of major crises with varying cultural resources and responses.

That truth in no way diminishes the validity of Sorokin's general terms, the dimensions of human nature and situationality being as they are. Given the human being's animality and adaptivity, the sensory experience of actuality has its central function; then human sociality implies normative role models with their ideality; and lastly, the whole complex thrust of history demands that those normatives have to be mythically buttressed and integrated. Naturally, then, it is a universal fact that sensate, idealistic, and ideational cultural expressions show themselves at all times.

However, this impression does not entail a succession of historic phases totally ruled by each cultural supersystem in turn. In point of fact, large movements and tendencies can be found here and there historically, but such trends admit of being thwarted by the matrix of cultural controls so that any cyclical pattern may be prevented.

For example, in Hindu culture, caste and the Brahminic ascendancy preserved a multitude of customs and values. Tight linkage between their religious scriptures and most of the dependent philosophies made for institutionalized continuity with the ideational. Specific differences made this less true of the West, where religion and philosophy have their separate origins from Jerusalem and from Athens. Consequently, religion and philosophy more readily diverge.

A joint Hindu defense by caste, religion, and philosophy, first against Buddhism and other early unorthodoxies, much later against Islamic and Western incursions, served to smother any possible movement toward sensate predominance.

Indian sensate values may have found a partial release while still submerged by the ideational, where they had been placed in the earlier stages of humanity spiritual career, not to mention their underground and symbolic expression in Tantric forms of belief.

Where China was concerned, the social and political role of Confucianism, closely tied to the structures imposed by an imperial government, assured its survival and relative fixity, as well as its natural disputes with the more other-worldly Taoism and Buddhism. Reactions against Buddhist movements, going along with security, prosperity, and impositions of imperial power, led to a greater flowering of sensate culture in China than in India.

At any rate, Confucianism preserves "idealism," in its exemplary sense. Recently, Western pragmatism and Marxism have worked to pull Chinese thought in a more sensate direction than Confucianism had allowed.

Following Sorokin, we can say that Western, Hindu, and Chinese civilizational phases are differently attuned by their respective dominant cultural controls, given the particularities of each. Sorokin's classifications of ideational, idealistic, and sensate, however simplified, throw considerable light on the various philosophies generated in these civilizations. But two qualifying provisos should be kept in mind: Sorokin's terms have a broader reference than the philosopher's typical "isms," and the particularities of major civilizations must not be forgotten in any generalizing effort. The following brief comments reinforce those qualifications.

In certain respects, perennial philosophical types occur across civilizational boundaries, which can be shown through an attempt to apply a Western-based typology to Eastern philosophies. Carvaka matches Western naturalism and skepticism. Vedanta (non-dualist, dualist, and qualified non-dualist), parallels Western non-naturalisms of monist, dualist, and mixed sorts. Vaisesika and Nyaya are atomistic realisms, though paying lip service to Upanishadic non-naturalism. Buddhist philosophies are withdrawal strategies, but mystical rather than skeptical. Here is the main difference between Western and Eastern philosophies. Though mystical withdrawal strategies are found in the West, in Plotinus for example, they are not there dominant, given that Western philosophies of the speculative sort project a rational envisagement into the very center of the myth; for example, Platonic forms, the Divine Intellect, the Logos, or the World Order. Preoccupation with rationally unfolding sciences and political orders, together with both philosophical and monotheistic abrogations of earlier pre-Axial mythic forms, allows the West a more freely projected rational envisagement, while the less scientific and more mythically and socially burdened East, especially India but also China with its Taoism, must seek "liberation" from its heavy legacy in a high supra-rational moment. Karl Potter used the theme of "liberation" as basic for this typology of Indian philosophies; this would not work for the West.

One basic point emerges: cultural and philosophical differences between East and West themselves help make a strong sensate turn unlikely in Hindu and Chinese cultures.

2. The West and East Compared

A Western typology of philosophical positions, while not wholly transferable without qualification to Eastern thought, can offer some advantages as a comparative frame for Eastern philosophies. Perennial types in some ways do reoccur across temporal and civilizational boundaries. For help in spelling this out, one may best look to underlying socio-cultural functions, according to the thought of Pitirim A. Sorokin.

Naturalism has been a constant in the West, as has skepticism. As remarked earlier, both of these match well enough with the heterodox Indian school of Carvaka. There are varied non-naturalisms in the West–dualism, monism, and mixed varieties–which have palpable affinities to the three major modes of Vedanta. For incidental support, one can appeal to Radhakrishnan, who argued that Indian thought permeated Hellenistic philosophy. In any event, a striking analogue does hold between Plotinus and Samkara, even though the question of specific influence does not here arise. Other similarities can be found in the comparison of Vaisesika and Nyaya to Western atomistic realisms, also those between idealist schools in Buddhism and Western idealisms, as well as those between Zen and existentialisms, along with resonances between Buddhist *anatta* and Humean phenomenalism.

Nonetheless, all this does not add up to typological uniformity. Major differences remain. Neither the classification traditionally used for schools of Indian thought nor Karl Potter's useful proposal that "liberation" is the key to the East correspond to any plausible system fitting Western philosophies (Potter 1972). This question has wide ramifications. One striking lapse is the failure of Sorokin's supersystemic oscillations to hold for Eastern civilizations as well as for the West. Sorokin's *Social and Cultural Dynamics* shows two clear cycles of the major rhythms for the West. However, in that work he often acknowledged that they are not uniform across civilizations, being less strong in the Chinese tradition and weaker yet in the Indian (vol. 4, pp. 770-71). As was said earlier, the religions and philosophies of the past were ideational. The most sensate was at best only rational idealism. Moreover, recent sensate elements in Indian thought may be Western imports or effects of those. We have noted that Kautalya's political philosophy, like that of the Chinese legal realist Yang Choo, matches the "cynical sensate" *Prince* of Machiavelli (Sorokin and Lunden 1959, p. 19). But such themes in Hinduism are decidedly secondary .

China differed in that ideational Taoism and the imported and locally transformed Buddhism contrasted sharply with the "mixed" or "idealistic" position of Confucianism. Rhythms in Chinese philosophy and art, with a sensate trend apparently cresting in the middle T'ang Dynasty (Cowell 1970, p. 59ff.), are far clearer than in India's.

Even these do not at all match Western swings towards sensate values in late classical and early modern times. Sorokin's specific views about Western philosophies can be usefully amplified.

3. Explanatory Rootages and Trends

The dominant cultural control system cannot prevent the coexistence of multiple philosophical types. A range always survives, though all do not prosper equally. Functionally speaking, there seem to be four constant rootages from which co-temporal perspectives arise. The major themes of Sorokin's supersystems seemed to match up with three of these rootages. The other manifests the inwardness pivotal for both ideational and idealistic creativity.

The first root lies in our practical sense of outwardness. This corresponds to sensate immediacies, or clues to the world and cues for action. Construe the next root as the sense of inward selfhood. This has no direct counterpart Sorokinian phase, but is crucial for two others: the ideational and the idealistic. It leads toward the foundational insight and gives the center for idealistic acknowledgments. This inward turn comes as a hailing—a recalling, a movement to the pivot for re-viewing and re-newing the values by which the self and the whole culture grow and endure. This inward turn is thus a basic moment for ideational and idealistic creation, sensate outwardness being inadequate for their generation.

The third root, the normative, is humanity's social and emulative sense, the awareness of patterned ways of life deserving both celebration and emulation. Idealistic culture leans upon guiding patterns in a socially selective manner, as in the importance of knightly and priestly role models. Finally, the fourth root is transcendentally based in humanity's religious sense. This involves the foundational insight, going beyond both worldly outwardness and the normative realm of social patterns.

Different selections from, and shapings of, all those rootages generate basic philosophical types. Naturalisms claim to follow outwardness. Traditional non-naturalisms, resembling religions but also gearing into the history of science and politics, grow from all the roots. In the case of dualism, a gap prevails between the first world-descriptive root and the other culturative three. In monism, a fusion between worldly and culturative factors is offered. Given Western secularization of thought, pushing the integrative foundational insight offstage, we find attenuated systems reflecting only the first three roots.

As we have seen in section 1, each perennial type falls into foreground *or* shadow depending upon sociocultural trends and their control systems. Supersystemic controls heighten the audibility of views in the current mode.

The West has been most vulnerable to supersystemic forces of change, but in the East it was otherwise. Historic reasons should be looked for to explain the difference. In Hindu culture, the Brahmin ascendancy and caste system preserved a multitude of customs and values. Tight linkage between Vedic scriptures and the dependent philosophies of the six orthodox schools assured continuity with the ideational. But in the West, religion and philosophy have separate origins in Jerusalem and Athens, and more readily diverge.

A joint Hindu defense by caste, religion, and philosophy against Buddhism and other unorthodoxies, later against Islamic and Western incursions, smothered any movement toward sensate predominance. Indian sensate values may have found partial release while submerged by the ideational, where they are indulged in the earlier stages of humanity's spiritual career, as well as in Tantric forms of belief.

In China, the social and political role of Confucianism, through structures imposed by the empire, assured survival and relative fixity as well as conflicts with Taoism and Buddhism. Worldly reactions against Buddhist movements, stimulated by renewed security, prosperity, and reinvigorated imperial power, led to a higher flowering of sensate culture than in India. Nonetheless, Confucianism preserved Idealism in its exemplary sense. Western imports of pragmatism and Marxism have recently worked to pull Chinese thought in a more sensate direction than Confucianism had earlier allowed.

4. Animism and East/West Differences

Among the origins of Western philosophy, animism should be noticed. Animism is ambiguous between the form in which centers of meaning come as separable from nature and that in which they are embedded in nature, one form leading to spirit worship, the other to nature worship. Those two trends pass through Orphism and Platonism, and through double-aspect monism in Stoicism. However, most forms of the tradition mix dualist and monist expressions. The impersonality in traditions of "philosophical faith" yields some affinities to Eastern thought and a relative contrast to Biblicism.

When this Western animist tradition becomes secularized, it still keeps partial continuity with earlier forms. Let these forms of animism be construed as strategies for placing man jointly within his world and normative culture, where the integrating foundational insight drops out of sight. The epistemological-logical reading of Indian thought made by Matilal seems closer to Western placement strategies than to non-naturalisms.

The metaphysical aspect is less central in both secularizing approaches, but natural enough since, as Stephen Katz remarked, "In Indian thought all metaphysics is soteriological" (1978, p. 58). Certainly, analytic philosophy can be given various expressions. A notion that ways of thought and talk have to be analyzed and clarified as the "begin-all" for philosophy evokes some echoes within Hindu and Buddhist thought. Sometimes, analysis of common sense or science leads to withdrawal strategies attempting to dis-integrate all well-founded placement strategies. Having earlier seen how Western phases follow Sorokin's oscillatory pattern better than those of the East, we return to the sharp contrast underlying Western and Eastern typologies. Great stress falls upon mystical withdrawal strategies in Indian and Chinese cultures. Neo-Platonism does reflect a mystical withdrawal strategy, yet as a minority current in the West. Why? The high standing of "rational envisionment" as an ideal goal for thought, rather than Eastern "liberation," downplays mysticism. Athens and Jerusalem jointly produced a view of an ultimate rational order. The Biblical God was personal; the Platonic Forms or Logos then projected upon the Divine Mind its ultimate characterizations. In contrast, those elements of order which started out from within Indian culture were Karma and Samsara. These were structural settings for the human situation, not ideal targets for worshipful attention.

Oddly enough, the origin of metaphors for non-naturalist rational envisionment had to be worldly envisionment, literally portrayed in the notion of a worldview. Yet, the worldview cannot in and of itself carry the full weight of mythic world description and culturation. Outward envisionment may be the true ideal of philosophical naturalists, but it demands symbolic transformation in order to initiate the culturative dynamic. This was achieved through a merger of Platonic rational envisionment and Biblical theology. Although one can not grasp the Divine Mind, an ultimately rational order (though exceeding human comprehension) was set before Western humanity. To the contrary, the "liberation" emphasis in the East betokened a cutting free from rational categories. Such mysticism was more suspect in the

West. So once again we see that the typology for Eastern philosophies proposed by Karl Potter would not fit philosophies of the West. Western anti-systems usually are more skeptical than mystical, partly since the communal religions of their area stress revelation more than reason. William of Ockham combined a skeptical anti-mystical or anti-metaphysical approach with Biblical fideism. Augustinianism more closely approached Neo-Platonism, but even here the ideal contemplative pattern is restricted to the elect within the Church Triumphant. Mystical withdrawal can never fulfill all the needs of orthodox believers or the mainline speculative metaphysicians, given the way they accentuate the Divine Reason.

Salvifics in Biblical traditions likewise differ from those of the East. The personal immortality so associated here permits of idealized rational envisionment, but *moksha,* or Nirvana, or identification with the Tao, burst the limits of any ordered contemplative rationality. Western scientific and political interest puts its premium upon the ultimate contemplation of rational order. The mutually involved orders of Karma and Samsara are to be escaped from, rather than ideally contemplated.

Western critical philosophy and monotheist Biblicism pruned back local primitive religious traces to a degree surpassing Eastern sublimations. Xenophanes and Plato led the attack against literary polytheism, while prophets and their successors contended against Baal and nature worship. All this allowed greater freedom in drawing up a rational envisionment pointing to the Divine. The conservative East was more tolerant of primordial beliefs and practices. Such richness of tradition might well have heightened the need for mystical escape from that multiplicity, and precluded any major alliance with science.

5. Toward a Balanced Perspectivism

To understand the melding of perspectives, each contributing phase needing its own reworking, we can reflect on dialectical synthesis. When some innovator accommodates multiple ways of life or thought to one another, s/he participates in more than one group and its norms, actually *or* through imaginative identification. If he does this through imaginatives identification, there could be a strain of "fortunate *mis*identification" pertaining to one or more of the mythic moments. This identification might suggest influence: "Plato must have read the books of Moses." Or it could be taken as a projected picture of destined confluence: "All religions are paths to the same goal."

In fact, the "fortunate" character of what literally may be a "misidentification" lies in functional analogues between the moments identified. Working on both sides with "live" symbolic options, the individual doing the synthesizing engages in culturative authorization and integration. Such engagements are taken as "higher" truths, "higher" than the level where different elements are distinguished. Nihilism refuses all such "higher" truths, claiming the number of cultural forms as grounds for dropping them all. "Synoptic" thinking thus cannot simply follow the outward world-descriptive function, but incorporates "mythic" culturative moments. Those count as invocations of the self, authorizings for ways of life and thought, and integrations and adjustments through a foundational insight. This larger perspective lends interest to theological reinterpretations of Hegel's thought.

Sound perspectivism must seek to maximize its scope, both back through time and across civilizational bounds. The quest for the One, portrayed by Copleston's Gifford lectures, presents an unbroken legacy for such maximization (Copleston 1982).

Perspectivism is implied by a perennialism of types (necessarily rough and imperfect) and by comparative philosophy. What are the virtues of healthy perspectivism? Simply the avoidance of two mortal diseases: fanaticism and nihilism. The arbitrariness of fanaticism and the aimlessness of nihilism are offenses against reason. Socrates fought mindless traditionalism and Sophism; Kant steered between dogmatism and skepticism; William James negotiated between idealist and scientistic "block-universes." In the thirties and forties, respectable thinkers worried about secular existentialisms and logical positivism. A sound perspectivism must and can seek balance through a sensible accounting for mythic components. This saves the appearances for non-naturalisms, which in turn allows the only promising junctures for Western and Eastern philosophies. Cross-civilizational scanning of myth, especially the sublimated kind, forces philosophers to face up to the many ways of life and thought, without falling into ideological fanaticism or scientific or romantic nihilism. Comparative religion and philosophy would find their best fulfillment under such perspectival construal, the sociocultural matrices for which are well sketched out by Sorokin. Cultural systems find more hopeful explanations with Dilthey and Sorokin than with positivists or ideologues or (partisan) theologians or metaphysicians; furthermore, those accounts must span East and West.

6. Concluding Observations

Religious faiths differ from "philosophical faiths," because of being preoccupied with extraordinary diagnostics and salvifics. All share common concern with an integrating foundational insight, although Buddhism, in some measure, counts as an exception. Unlike religions, philosophies put their trust in autonomous reason. Objections to rational vain-glory rise especially from Biblical traditions: "Reason is the Devil's whore!" exclaimed Luther. Such communal faiths attend to the depths of the human predicament, the heights of Divine Holiness, and so to the need for revelatory assistance. Targeting and authorizing moments in religions are less salient than in philosophical faiths, given their more intense diagnostics and salvifics. Speculative functions demand autonomy in Western thought because of collateral scientific and political business. Speculation is less structured in the East. There, the mystical strategy can go to greater dis-integrative extremes while preserving the religious function. For example, in Buddhism diagnostic replaces inwardness and salvific the foundational insight.

Western philosophy can be set against Eastern in two basic respects. Its roots are less identified with communal faiths than are Indian and Chinese philosophies, Athens not being Jerusalem. Secondly, Western philosophy from the classic period on was engaged with nascent sciences and with political institutions. Insofar as it carried on its inherited animist substance and mythic form, these sharply transformed features made up a guiding matrix for growing science and political thought. That guiding role did not preclude interaction with religion, but led to greater methodological self-consciousness, often at odds with the mythic. Nowadays, methodological concerns with science and discourse downplay any mythic elements promoting culturation and integration of ways of life.

Karl Jaspers's treatment of "philosophical faiths" transcends specialist and marginal preoccupations by showing the realms where West and East can illumine analogous functions. Sorokin's transcultural treatments of the ideational and idealistic do the same. Perspectivism should prosper from joint appreciation of myth and method in *all* major philosophical traditions. That Western methods are more consciously pursued, while Eastern forms are more deeply anchored socially in old traditions, is relatively unimportant. Basic family resemblances span all the civilizational bounds.

PART THREE

SOROKIN ON MODERNITY

Eleven

CROCE AND SOROKIN ON LIBERALIZATIONS

This chapter compares Croce and Sorokin respecting their views on freedom in history. These two thinkers, one an adherent of "rough dialectics" and the other of "progressive dialectics," have more in common: a shared admiration of Giambattista Vico's "corsi i recorsi," a use of Hegel, and considerable political courage against political tyrannies. But Croce's liberalism, like that of Kerensky, is at some distance from Sorokin's "conservative Christian anarchism." Croce was a distinguished member of a group of European philosophers ably dealing with issues of culture and history, and reflecting Kantian and Hegelian influences.

Furthermore, Croce is a member of the "cloud of witnesses" we can call upon to mediate between John Herman Randall, Jr., and Pitirim A. Sorokin regarding the nature of cultural creativity. He also provides a useful bench mark in considering Sorokin's interesting ambivalence on liberalism.

> Philosophy, when it inquires and interprets . . . observes with serenity how periods of increased or reduced liberty follow upon each other and how a liberal order, the more it is established and undisputed, the more surely decays into habit, and thereby its vigilant self-awareness and readiness for defense is weakened, which opens the way for a recourse, as Vico termed it, to all of those things which seemed to have vanished from the world, and which themselves, in their turn, open a new course. (Croce 1955, p. 58)

This passage from Croce reminds us of the oscillations in freedom, both long-term and short-term, cited by Pitirim A. Sorokin in his *Social and Cultural Dynamics* (1957, pp. 487ff, 509ff.). But the reminder misleads if too much is read into it. As a historian, Croce distrusts over-schematic patterns of order that are given by "philosophers of history" (Spengler or Toynbee, or even Vico himself). Sorokin's framework, subtly qualified though it is, retains much of a positivist legacy despite its Neo-Platonic transformation. Furthermore, as a Western European, Croce draws selectively upon "speculative romanticism." He would purge Hegel of his systematic excesses, while leaving the "story of liberty" as history's central theme and affirming his hero Vico's contribution—the idea that philosophy properly reflects upon historiography.

Croce scrutinizes particularities of a political, literary, and philosophical culture moving back toward their origins and forward toward their subtle interplays with circumstances and rival idealities. Sorokin, by contrast, though grudgingly admiring early nineteenth century accomplishments, stands at a distance. He takes cultural particularities less for their own sake than as "for-instances" supportive of his oscillations theory. He also is suspicious of what he takes as "voluntarism," so widespread in modern European thought. In Sorokin's terms, though not in everyone's, Croce might be labelled a voluntarist. At any rate, despite agreeing with Croce on cultural and political phenomena they both deplore, Sorokin illustrates sharply a civilizational contrast with Western Europe. This contrast appears in his clash with derivative American thinkers. Nonetheless, both men offer correctives, though from different angles, for our reflections on freedom. In what follows, Croce's and Sorokin's accounts of freedom's waxings and wanings will be sketched out. Next, a brief search for pure cases of such oscillations will be pursued in a sceptical vein. Finally, I shall suggest the uses, as antidotes to ideology, to which we should put Croce and Sorokin.

1. Croce Center-Stage

Much relevant material by Croce is available in English translation: *A History of Italy from 1871-1915* (1940), *A History of the Kingdom of Naples* (1963), and *History as the Story of Liberty* (1970). A. Robert Caponigri provides us an excellent study, *History and Liberty: the Historical Writings of Benedetto Croce* (1955).

These works show Croce as a deeply involved historian and commentator upon modernity. His "philosophy of spirit" descends from formulations given in more technical and abstract works, while his special place in Italian life and thought becomes clear. For Croce, liberalism is rightly "the religion of liberty," not "economic liberalism" or *laissez-faire*. It strikes Croce as ethical in its essence, and the freedom which it sponsors is more a matter of spiritual creativity than of economic arrangements (Croce 1962, p. 30ff.). But liberalism stands continually at odds with competing "religious" principles; Jacobin democracy, absolutism, clericalism, communism, and national imperialisms being examples. The nineteenth century has allowed the greatest successes for liberalism so far. On this point, Croce and Sorokin would cordially agree, although Sorokin sees the high point of "sensate freedom" as beginning a long slide downward (Sorokin and Lunden 1959, p. 138). Croce emphatically does not concur. To take setbacks for freedom as bound up with long-term sociocultural rhythms would be "pessimistic," since Croce's anticlericalism certainly innoculates him against Sorokin's enthusiasms for "ideational" or religious recovery.

No "pessimist" then, while admitting the twentieth century has buffeted badly the ideal of freedom, Croce takes such declines not as necessitated but as resulting from ethical failures. Nationalisms and irrationalisms before and after the first World War had followed upon positivistic (and hence "pessimistic") underminings of idealism in the latter nineteenth century. Fascism, as Caponigri points out, was not regarded by Croce as predetermined (Caponigri 1955, pp. 90ff.). Contingent human weaknesses of intellectuals and political leaders, largely inspired by the unfortunate German example, led to tyrannical results. Spiritual unrest played its part.

> Industrialism and Bismarckism, with their repercussions and internal struggles, were unable to create a new and satisfying religion; but they had produced an uneasy condition of mind, a combination of lust for enjoyment, the spirit of adventure and of joy in conquest, frantic craving after power, restlessness and with a lack of enthusiasm and indifference, a state of mind that must be looked for in a life lived divorced from its center, that center being for man his moral and religious consciousness. . . . It was in the atmosphere prepared by D'Annunzio and by the growth of a plutocratic psychology, that delights in things outwardly dazzling and fundamentally gross, that the philosophy of reac-

> tion against positivism developed in Italy.
> (Croce 1963, p. 240)

In short, thought and culture gone astray greatly disarranges political life. With this account of declining intelligence and morale, analogous to the "sentimental romanticism" of the nineteenth century, Croce notes the conditions wherein the accident of Fascism could take its rise. (Another contingency was the monarch's weakness of will before the "March on Rome.")

Parenthetically, such conditions of decay leading to loss of liberty match up closely with the "overripe sensate" stage inveighed against by Sorokin. One difference of emphasis is that Sorokin also addresses questions of broad social morale, for instance, in *The American Sex Revolution* (1957). Croce more nearly confines his polemical attention to cultural, intellectual, and political matters. Perhaps he felt the Roman Catholic Church would monitor morality in Italy. It should be left with something to do after forfeiting the Papal States, he might think.

Where Croce discussed decadence (loss of freedom), he chose to treat it as a "failure of ethical will." Surely this does not fit the Sorokinian sociocultural explanation in terms of broad value crisis. But while Croce is more individualistic and Sorokin more sociological, both focus on values and on thought. Some reinforcements between the two should be possible.

The triadic sociocultural framework of Sorokin would be unwelcome to Croce, as well as his predilection to admire ideational ages. Nonetheless, both men share "favorite hatreds," ranging from artistic colossalisms, futurisms, and irrational romanticisms, to positivisms, naturalisms, and state socialisms. Where Croce anatomized Marxism and Fascism, Sorokin debated Trotsky and anathematized state tyrannies. Neither man could ever be accused of conformism. While each was rooted in different cultures, and came from different social strata, both addressed matters of twentieth century decay and folly. Their angles of vision differ; Sorokin takes the much longer view. But they agree in finding some virtues in the nineteenth century, aspects of which are badly threatened today.

For Sorokin, the largest scale rhythms for freedom amount to crises attending the development and overthrow of sociocultural "supersystems," "ideational," "idealistic," *and* "sensate." Furthermore, Sorokin distinguishes between fundamental types of freedom appropriate to each supersystem. His explanatory model for this strikes one as excessively simple, being a ratio between the sum of wishes and the sum of available means (Sorokin 1957, pp. 88f.). That formula's merits include highlighting contrasting moral psychologies and changing life strategies marking persons undergoing rapid social mobility. It accomplishes less toward clarifying the social and political dimensions of freedom. Sensate freedom involves maximizing the sum of means to match the sum of wishes; ideational freedom reduces the wishes to match the means; the mixed (or idealistic) type both expands means and reduces wishes. It all reminds one of Mr. Micawber's advice on thrift to David Copperfield upon his entering the Fleet debtors' prison, or the advice of John Wesley: "Earn all you can; save all you can; give all you can." Perhaps Sorokin was still fascinated with Tolstoyan ideals in designing his model.

More directly to the point are the judgments Sorokin makes regarding "short-term fluctuations" affecting liberalizations and their contraries: he lists "(1) War or peace, (2) Impoverishment or prosperity, and (3) Social emergency of any kind" as factors affecting the degree of freedom (1957, pp. 484ff.). Can this be rejected as too commonplace to deserve mention? I think not, since both Neo-Manchesterian and Marxist thought studiously ignore the obvious in their respective Utopianisms. Sorokin's critique of today's sensate culture would not allow fashionable ideologues to escape so easily. Incidentally, our present crisis involves both long-term and short-term factors reducing human freedom. Sorokin's total scheme needs various qualifications, and Croce's historical story needs rounding out. At any rate, examples can be given which are consistent with Croce's and Sorokin's story, in short cycles toward and away from freedom.

What counts as a liberalization? Again, what sorts of liberalization are there? Next, what cases reasonably show us clear movements between increased and decreased freedom? Exploring these questions first from our own perspective, and second from those of Croce and Sorokin, should help us compare and test their theories. We assume liberalization to be a giving or a taking of greater freedom. "Freedom in what respect?" yields us a principle for distinguishing the several sorts. Accordingly, liberalizations exist for enhanced political roles, economic well-being, or for social and cultural options.

The most prominent examples are political. The nineteenth century surely, and the twentieth century sporadically, have seen political freedom enlarged. Extensions of freedom fall under two heads: widening of the franchise and return to national from foreign control. Croce approves both, finding the "ascension . . . of strata to political participation" to be one positive side of "true" (that is, liberalized or domesticated) "socialism" (Caponigri 1955, p. 241), and taking Italy's Risorgimento and unification as the crowning nineteenth century liberal success.

As for cycles under the sub-heading of widening the franchise, there are times when broadened franchises effectively undo their liberal intent, by slippages into plebiscitory autocracies. The case of Louis Napoleon's election and imperial role, the collapse of the Weimar republic, and other instances, such as those criss-crossing with the subheading of national liberations, come to mind. I recall Carlos Romulo's speech at Harvard advising Americans not to be surprised if democracy failed to flower in the Pacific basin. African and South American states also have often lost their democratic form. Croce showed liberalism to be continually at odds with contrary tendencies; that illumined the problem to some degree. Add to that Sorokin's discussion of the factors influencing short-term fluctuations, and particularly his comments on the liberalizing/autocratic pattern found in revolutions. These patterns in revolutions may be a special case of the general cycle, under the cynical direction of those holding revolutionary leadership, *first* to overthrow and *then* to clamp on an even more Draconian mastery.

In this country, the Civil Rights movement partakes of political and economic modes. Its equivocal success in the economic realm, and to a lesser degree, that of Women's Liberation as well, points to the tremendous potential for backlash from interests and from social conservatism. Nonetheless, both movements have somewhat advanced their causes, backlash or no; and given the needs of the nation and its economy, it is perhaps high time. (This is supposition merely, but Croce could have detected traces of Jacobin egalitarianism in *some* of the rhetoric of these two movements. The elections of 1994 suggest an organized backlash, perhaps reminiscent of the 1876 ending of Reconstruction.)

Cultural and moral "liberation," products of the turbulent sixties, would have impressed Sorokin as tending toward license rather than toward freedom. Standards of public utterance, publication, and behavior, have been condoned in ways best described as "overripe sensate," where the customer (whatever he or she wants) is always right. Backlash has been generated here so as to strengthen reactions against worthier goals. Neither Jacobin democracy nor communism lead to freedom, and Croce's liberalism also serves as an effective check to those views. He excludes "economic liberalism," which preeminently falls under Sorokin's anti-sensate critique. Since Americans now take *laissez-faire* as one pillar of conservatism, and since Sorokin's analysis of freedom's short-term fluctuations shows the combined assumptions of jerry-built conservatism wildly askew, his own "cultural conservatism" provides a good antidote.

The two poles of Neo-Manchesterian and modified Marxist ideologies illustrate the motivating extremes in American political life. Although Daniel Bell's pronouncement of the "end of ideology" was no doubt wrong, the vaguest of pragmatisms have come to occupy the middle ground of political thought. Ideologies lack the political wisdom shown by Croce's history and Sorokin's sociology. In their dynamics they push constituencies now leftward, now rightward. Croce and Sorokin both seriously examine thought and values and how they work in history. Raw materialism, implied by both Manchesterian and Marxist views, allows room for neither human freedom nor creativity.

Twelve

SOROKIN AND TOYNBEE

Arnold Toynbee's Centennial year was also in 1989. He too was a formative influence for the International Society for the Comparative Study of Civilizations and his participation, along with Sorokin's, at the first meeting in Salzburg was crucial.

Carle Zimmermann and others have wisely emphasized the common ground in the historical sociology of both scholars: Sorokin on crisis, Toynbee on "challenge-and-response," and both on spiritual and cultural creativity. Those themes reinforce one another. Whereas Sorokin drew on Comte, Tolstoy, and Kropotkin, Toynbee highlighted Thucydides, Gibbon, and Augustine. However wide-ranging their sources and chosen fields, both scholars spoke to many of the same intellectual needs properly felt by the educated twentieth-century public.

This set of notes is meant to affirm the high roles of, and affinities between, Toynbee and Sorokin in civilizational study, their present-day relevancy, and the subtlety of their interactions. The areas of overlap between them, once their differences are rightly conceded, are indeed substantial. Each man produced mountains of material in civilizational research.

Where do we best look for illumination on these scholars? For Sorokin, the volume edited by Philip Allen, *Pitirim A. Sorokin in Review* (1963), contains late reflections and answers to critics as well as an insightful collegial essay by Toynbee. Also, there is Sorokin's *Sociological Theories of Today* (1966), especially chapters 7 and 8 bearing on Toynbee and other peers. Then we should check *The Problems of Civilizations* (1964), edited by Othmar Anderle, presenting the classic and original exchanges from Salzburg. This has much from both Toynbee and Sorokin; the latter especially gives a consensual overview of their shared ground on pages 55-56. (In 1941, Sorokin had given some early responses to critics of volumes 1-3, in his fourth volume of *Social and Cultural Dynamics*).

On Toynbee, I recommend not only Ashley Montague's *Toynbee and History* (1956) for analysis, but also Toynbee's volume 12 of his

A Study of History: Reconsiderations (1961) for considered responses. *Toynbee on Toynbee* (1974) is more conversational in tone, but has at least one last good-humored but revealing observation on Sorokin.

Sorokin and Toynbee, like Spengler but far more shrewdly, had gathered vast reams of data in ways that led Westerners to take broader views of history and culture. And high time it was for this, the twentieth century being what it is. Their groupings of the data stimulated vigorous responses often of lasting worth.

Toynbee has much to offer the civilizational de-limiters and definers; the International Society for the Comparative Study of Civilizations "boundaries" scholars manifestly carry his brand. On the other hand, comparative study has to look for typological aspects, large culturological factors made intelligible by their underpinnings in social changes and convulsions. Sorokin serves us well in the raising of such issues.

With Sorokin, "Worldviews," their intense crises, and sometimes drastic transformations, make sense, particularly, in light of stresses between "Central Civilization" (or its would-be rival claimants) and the outlands. As a philosopher of "perspectival" leanings (and what other leanings are possible for a member of a comparative civilization group?), I find Sorokin's account of culture one of the few which makes any sense of major shifting trends. Beyond this, I find both Sorokin and Toynbee have much to give, well-based upon prodigious data, concerning the point and purpose of civilizational study, namely creative accommodations and survival strategies. Rather than contest the respective greatnesses of Toynbee and Sorokin, I claim that Toynbee's influence has been mostly felt heretofore, as in our group's "boundaries" sessions and Matt Melko's and Leighton Scott's resulting volume, while Sorokin's will yet be shown as pertaining to the conditions for "Worldview" clashes and transmutations.

One additional note: a feasible defense of Sorokin's alleged "dogmatism," and of his quantified tables in *Social and Cultural Dynamics* can be offered. For one thing, Sorokin's writings can be sorted into those intended for popular readership, those for a general, well-educated audience, and those for specialists. Qualifications are best expressed in the latter two sorts and were to be found most clearly in late writings. For another thing, Sorokin was often engaged in simultaneous polemics and defense, for which self-assurance was undoubtedly the best stance. As regards his use of statistics, one might give a sharp twist to John Herman Randall, Jr.'s attribution of satiric intent, his sly "He must have been kidding" theme. Sorokin, if we could imagine him to be kidding, was rather "kidding on the square," being quite serious about his substantive claims, perhaps less so about the details. *Formally*, his use of statistics on qualitative readings of culture may be overdrawn but he did mark trends as measured by data, the characteristics of which are manifestly shown as changing. These chartings generally supported well the oscillations his sociocultural theory proclaimed.

Thirteen

REFLECTIONS UPON SOROKIN

This informal chapter updates a promotional handout announcing the Centennial programs honoring Sorokin, joined with a similarly relaxed discussion of Talcott Parsons, whose view counts as sublimated Protestantism or rational liberalism, under the shadow of Kant and Weber, and certainly as progressive dialectic. (John Herman Randall, Jr., also sublimated his inherited Protestantism, but in the Deweyan direction of empiricist liberalism.) Begrudgingly perhaps, Sorokin had noted similarities between his approach and Parsons's approach to social and cultural systems.

The following thoughts were meant as pump-priming for myself regarding Sorokin's Centennial and the proper International Society for the Comparative Study of Civilizations recognition thereof. They may be of some use to fellow scholars likewise engaged in study and reassessments of Sorokin's full legacy.

I want to follow up a line that Edward Tiryakian once pursued during an insightful plenary Comparative Civilizations presentation some years ago about the shifting center of civilizational creativity. This shift was again of specific interest to us in our 1989 meeting at Berkeley, given one thematic emphasis upon Pacific Rim cultures. Sorokin, in his Introduction to the one-volume edition of *Social and Cultural Dynamics,* referred to an "epochal shift" as the "first basic sociocultural process of the last four decades" (1957, p. xxiii). Attention was also paid to this movement away from Western Europe in his *Modern Historical and Social Philosophies* (1950, p. 298). There, he affirmed a consensual point shared by him with many of those writers he treats: "the coming civilization or culture is going to be basically different from that which has been dominant during the last five or six centuries." He continued: "I consider the vast region of the Pacific as the territorial center and the Americas, India, China, Japan, and Russia as the leading players in the coming drama of the emerging Integral and Ideational culture." For a more thorough treatment of the same general position see *The Basic Trends of Our Times* (Sorokin 1964, chap. 2). So much for one major aspect of prescience in Sorokin's work.

Refinements must be made in interpretations of Sorokin's overall role. Certainly many of his stances and critiques were highly controversial. My first presentation to the International Society for the Comparative Study of Civilizations, which eventuated as "Sorokin vs. American Thought" (Talbutt 1980), was correct as far as it went–that Sorokin was reacting intensely against his own earlier Westernizing progressivism and that he could not understand or appreciate fully the dominant ethos of American academic life, itself deeply committed to an upbeat reading of modernization.

More must be said about the sympathetic echoes Sorokin elicited in the provinces and the outlands (including other civilizations) while he was infuriating secular Cosmopolitans by attacks upon "overripe sensate" culture. "Passive sensate" and "cynical sensate" values are certainly manifest in much contemporary urban life, both in the pursuits of the "undeserving poor" and those of the "idle rich," and markedly with those powerful individuals who betray their trust for gain. Nonetheless, one could hold that genuine urban values, such as those the knowledge-based professionals follow in their ideals of public service, are still largely in place. Indeed, Talcott Parsons, who dramatically differed from Sorokin in his Weberian-derived reading of modernity, stands as the defender of the upbeat account of urban possibilities, and therefore as a far more sympathetic role model for professional sociologists, whose services are more inevitably rendered to urban-type administrators than to anyone else. "His bread I eat, his song I sing."

Yet, consider the polarity in the radial contrariety between power centers and peripheries which is the basis for empathetic reaction or "psychic mobility" of the American spirit. Such resonances of movement are awakened to pioneer virtues, "getting away from it all," primary relationships as palpably more manifest in small communities, inherited religious and family values, Jefferson, Andrew Jackson, Bryan and the Populists, Mark Twain, Will Rogers, and recently Garrison Keillor, who drew millions back from *quiche* to "hot dish." Keillor, his regional friends Jean Redpath and Chet Atkins, together with (the fictive) Clarence Bunsen, more decisively outclassed Ed Meese, Ed Koch, Donald Trump, and Ivan Boesky among suburbanite public radio listeners than anything imaginable this side of Joshua's victory. Consider, on a trivial level, "Hee Haw's" outlasting Rowan and Martin's "Laugh-in," the tremendous ratings for "Return to Mayberry," and Andy Griffith's subsequent grafting of the Sam Ervin-type "country lawyer" persona upon the Perry Mason role in "Matlock."

On a different note, consider the back-handed damnation through faint praise that provincials accord the city, with all its corruption and turmoil. "It's a nice place to visit, but I wouldn't want to live there." Certainly that is more polite than Barry Goldwater's "Saw it off and let it float out to sea."

Now the contrarieties deep-set within the American psyche, magnetized alternatively by promotional urban recruitment, and by principled regional reaction to corruption, are not at all points identical to the polarities suggested by Sorokin in his long-range theory of sensate, ideational, and idealistic oscillations. Tolstoy and pan-Slavic thought stand at some distance from our own provincial idealisms; yet some bridging is possible and the vigor of Sorokin's rhetoric, not to mention the breadth of his supportive data and the realism of his accounts of cosmopolitan breakdowns, came across to interested parties. The truth of it is, whatever the differences among provincials and their values, they have more in common as contraries to any putative urban power, with its formal hierarchies of courtiers, bureaucrats, or organization men. Jean Redpath, with her ancestry from north of Hadrian's Wall, the Tenneseean Chet Atkins, Woebegoners who talk Minnesotan, not to mention the peanut farmer from Plains, do have in common the fact that none of them are city slickers or Yuppies. Nor, of course, was Pitirim A. Sorokin. The continued dynamic of anti-urban criticism, severely rejected as anti-intellectual by such earnest urban scholars as Richard Hofstadter and Morton White, can only have been re-fueled by credibility gaps–for example Watergate, Iran-Contra, insider trading, and Pentagon corruption, not to mention other manifestations of social deterioration–symptoms of which are displayed by the media in a remarkable mixture of feigned concern and self-conscious voyeurism.

The trajectories of two remarkable careers had crossed in 1937, and yet, whatever ensued from Talcott Parsons's favorably regarded *Structure of Social Action* (1937) and from Sorokin's sweeping and controversial *Social and Cultural Dynamics* should not make us concentrate solely on the dramatic academic rivalry. The backgrounds, attitudes, and professorial styles of the two men could not be more different. Sorokin was the son of an itinerant workman, and his academic junior, Parsons, was the son of a college president. Sorokin was a "lone wolf" and imperial in the high-flown European academic style; Parsons an all-too effective roller of logs in the American manner. The long-term consequences of their interactions were rich in irony for both.

One can well believe that aggravation, like grains of sand getting into oyster shells, has more to do with the generation of vigorous and novel scholarly production than do the carrots and sticks wielded by Deans. Sorokin's aggravations included moral indignation at Czarists and Bolsheviks, and he turned them at the progressivism and parochialisms of American scholarly trends. In his turn, Parsons was not sufficiently appreciated by Sorokin, who was tone-deaf to Kantian and Weberian themes. Both men held far wider visions of the tasks of social science than did their contemporaries, but Parsons's was one capable of assimilation by urban sociologists and their administrative patrons. His approach, while quite ambitious, was more plausibly marketable in America than was Sorokin's.

Parsons used the term "philosopher" not favorably but invidiously of Sorokin, and felt his influence to be quite unfortunate. (The irony in this lies in Parsons being himself very much a philosopher of social science, and of modern society; Max Weber, one of his sources, had been praised as a philosopher by the distinguished Karl Jaspers.) Sorokin was sympathetic to philosophers of culture and history, especially to those ignored by establishments. He thereby made himself vulnerable. The disadvantage of "lone wolf" status is the likelihood of being outnumbered. Parsons allied himself with other scholars, first at Harvard, and then at Chicago. The Department of Social Relations was the eventual local result in Cambridge. Given that Sorokin's relative isolation left him with time on his hands, and given the older theme of "social ethics" as one humble residual tradition in the department, James Conant's being the Pharaoh who kneweth not Pitirim was a blessing in disguise. That blessing was the giving of time for Sorokin's Creative Altruism research, backed by Eli Lilly since the late 1940s.

One can suggest that perhaps not all the dragon's teeth sown by Sorokin have yet sprouted, given the continuing trends since his day. This thought must be paired and balanced with the observation that Talcott Parsons's affirmations of genuine urban values, those of rational professional service or modernizations of Protestant "vocations," can be seen as more complementary than contradictory to Sorokin's affirmations of provincial standards and critiques of urban decadence. Whatever the contrast between their overall evaluations, their axiological commendations can be seen to cohere, in that today's corruptions would have been condemned roundly by both. Questionable ideological stances, sociobiology, and naive behaviorisms would likewise fall very short by the standards of both those great scholars.

Let me go further. Ancient China stood in need of both Confucius and Lao-tse; Revolutionary colonies needed both Hamilton and Jefferson; Russia found Counts Sergei Witte and Leo Tolstoy most relevant to her early pre-World War I needs; and, by analogy, today's sociocultural questions call for answers from Talcott Parsons and Pitirim A. Sorokin. And this is not a simple matter of splitting the differences, but of observing and following their real strengths. Considerable care is needful, but the rewards of such discrimination are high.

One additional set of comments pertain to the materials Sorokin offers for comparative civilizational study. The one-volume abridgment of *Social and Cultural Dynamics* contains suggestive leads no doubt, but fuller accounts of Eastern civilizational values–with their deep affinities to Idealistic and Ideational typologies–must be sought in the full four volumes. There is a slight obscuring of that aspect as Sorokin draws more data from Western history than from the East; however, Sorokin vigorously pursues analogies and affinities across the cultures. An interesting indirect rootage for Sorokin's broad sympathies lies in the thought of Tolstoy, declared heretical by the Russian Orthodox Church for his departures from Christian doctrine. The simplified or even generalized brand of mysticism set forth by the Russian sage gains in transmissibility to the East, as does Sorokin's interpretive follow-up. Lawrence T. Nichols has translated Sorokin's 1914 "L. N. Tolstoy as a Philosopher," and this source bears witness to Tolstoy's lasting impact on Sorokin's truly ecumenic philosophy of values. F. R. Cowell commented rightly that Sorokin contributes to cultural axiology, just as Joseph Ford emphasized Sorokin's pursuit of sociology "in conjuncture with philosophy."

Other prime sources include, but are not limited to, the aforementioned *Modern Historical and Social Philosophies* and the proceedings from the Salzburg meeting of the International Society for the Comparative Study of Civilizations, *Problems of Civilizations* (1964). Professor Hallen's article on the relevancy of Sorokin to Indian thought in his *Sorokin and Sociology* (1972) is quite apposite to the discussion as well. It attests to the sympathetic reverberations awakened by Sorokin in civilizations outside the West, and therefore bears upon and enriches comparative issues.

Fourteen

DIALECTIC AGAINST MODERNITY

A shorter version of this chapter, entitled "Sorokin's Challenge to Modernity," appears in Sorokin and Civilization (1995), *edited by Joseph Ford, M. Richard, and P. Talbutt. This* Festschrift *contains Centennial papers from the International Society for the Comparative Study of Civilizations. I am indebted to the publishers of Transactions Books for permission to use this material. Several presentations had been made, both at Hampton University in 1988, and at Berkeley in 1989, from which this material was drawn.*

There are two big pieces of the puzzle here. One gives more detail on the Parsons/Sorokin relation than is offered in Chapter Thirteen, "Reflections Upon Sorokin." The other is the full development of the "radial contrariety" vector which I regard as basic to placing Sorokin against both the American and the modernist background. As a coordinate, it works differently in Russian and American contexts, and Sorokin's rough dialectic runs entirely counter to urban-oriented progressivism. Yet American nostalgia for the hinterland gives Sorokin a precarious foothold to present his argument.

1. Contrarieties

Culturologists, like philosophers, deal with a multitude of values. Of these, some are contrary to one another, and some of these polar contrarieties usefully establish vectors for the charting of value change. One such opposition we can call "radial" since it is a function of the radius extending from power centers outward toward hinterlands and outlands. This serves as an interpretive schema that illumines Sorokin's regional background, his dialectic against the power centers of modernity in their overripe sensate corruption, and also his equivocal reception by colleagues. Contrarieties, radial and otherwise, can be projected metaphorically as vectors marking distances, that is, as differences between values.

"Vertical contrarieties," whether of economic or social status, are essentially metaphorical and had been such well before Sorokin developed his analysis of "social mobility." Such uses vary as to how metaphorical they seem. Some are more standard or apparently technical; for example, upper, middle, and lower class. Some are more colorful; Trollope's social-climbing Mrs. Lookaloft, Howells's *Rise of Silas Lapham,* and the Wheel of Fortune. "Upstairs; Downstairs," the British mini-series also has its literal sense, as indeed does what Sorokin called "horizontal mobility." The latter is something perfectly obvious; the physical movement of an individual to take another position of comparable economic and social status.

All such contrarieties constitute value contrasts, and a radial contrariety differs from any vertical one, social or economic, in suggesting actual distance, rather than metaphorical "social distance," between superiors and subordinates. Power centers, whose power is amplified by modern science, draw in wealth and talent from the provinces, and oftentimes the vectors between center and peripheries operate in interactive, symbiotic ways. The dominant psychic movement in America, for example, affirms "citifying" values, including the acquisition of academic skills for ascending the ladder to success. On the other hand, radial contrarieties can have their rough or adversarial, and mutually resistant aspects, and this latent feature of American culture is just the one to which Sorokin's major critique of modernity, inaugurated with *Social and Cultural Dynamics* made its strongest appeal. For some, he rocked the boat unpleasantly; for others, his data and ideas were more congenial. We can now illustrate and analyze such disaffinities and affinities, which, for Americans, often interact with the better-known vertical contrarieties of social and economic class.

2. American Reactions to Sorokin

After Sorokin threw down the gauntlet to modernity and its urban values in *Social and Cultural Dynamics*, he accomplished little more among modernists than gaining a reputation for raising uncomfortable questions (Tibbs 1943). The cards he held as presumptions and results of research made for no winning hand for the games most social science professionals wanted to play. Yet, he managed his own special cards adroitly enough in the eyes of admiring hinterland and outland observers, especially those tolerant of taking long-term views.

Sorokin's massively supported analysis and fierce critique of the "overripe sensate" deterioration gave a shock to modernity which sets a challenge to interpreters trying to grasp its origins and results. Sorokin drew widely upon remarkable historical resources and had a significant effect upon some readers, as when activating his polemical skills. Yet, his main venture did not have proportionate effects within the bastions of professional sociology. How and why this equivocal set of responses took place is part of the problem of interpreting Sorokin's significance.

Attractions towards Sorokin's frame of reference can be detected among persons with strong rural and regional values. This appears with the book which he co-authored with Carle Zimmermann, himself an American rural sociologist, *The Principles of Rural-Urban Sociology*. The difference between claims on behalf of the city and those on behalf of the countryside, or other less urbanized regions, were mostly resolved in favor of the countryside. In fact, the end of the book pointed out the dangers of "over-urbanization," clearly anticipating Sorokin's critique of "overripe sensate" culture. Sorokin's personal regional roots in the Komi people and his identification with the peasant party, rather than with urban Marxists, shaped the political alignments of his early life, his underlying values, and the cultural preferences expressed in his scholarship.

The American background is an interesting mix, and it engages with Sorokin's peripheralist attack upon urban centers by evoking its latent hinterlander side. At issue is more where Americans feel that they come from, rather than where Cosmopolis is apt to draw them, in seeking their fortune in the Big City. (Such drives toward success dominate urban sociologists, who serve administrators within "Central Civilization." The most basic, elementary sociology of knowledge supports that claim.) The vector connecting the hinterlands and urban power centers gives most of the powerful dynamic of American history and culture, even allowing for different operative forces from the economic and generational urban vectors cited by Marx and Freud. Sorokin heightened self-awareness and the sense of older values at the periphery among inveterate regionalists, an awareness not to be mistaken for simple nostalgia.

Generally speaking, they share positive symbiotic, but also adversarial, bondings (Cosmopolis interacting with its peripheries.) The "rurbifying" symbiotic links develop from mutually advantageous interchanges, and the negative relations from conflicting interests and incompatible patterns of self-esteem. Cosmopolis's inner peripheries, which are chiefly under its control, are the hinterlands occupied by "country cousins" (whose usual worldview is an older version of that remnant held at the center) or by not fully assimilated conquered or immigrant groups. The outer peripheries, or outlands, may or may not be within the same civilizational horizon, thus complicating the problem further for the scholar. They can be reached by traveling merchants (as in current forms of "neocolonialism"), missionaries, and not infrequently by punitive expeditions, with gunboats or other means, that are dispatched whenever the natives become excessively restless and disobedient.

With respect to Americans, our ancestors, from their peripheral location, assumed a brave adversarial attitude against their home power center, Great Britain. As colonists, pioneers, and settlers, they set about to vindicate their own special virtues and defend their principles. This sort of defiant celebration was continued in post-revolutionary times by hinterlanders within the nation, this time against political and economic dominance by the Northeast. Regionalist impulses toward secession were soon expressed in the nineteenth century, conspicuously culminating with the Civil War. Radial contrarieties, expressing themselves through intense "rurbification"—the mutual interaction between urban centers and outer regions—have ranged historically from a comparatively mild self-definition in regional literature, through irony regarding urban pretense, to explicit attack (as in Bryan's "Cross of Gold" speech). Politically, our federal institutions allow ample room for such energetic interplay, as do our literature, drama, journalism, and popular entertainments.

Examples of such adversarial veins throughout our culture are symptoms of deep-seated permeation of a radial contrariety between city and region, accordingly, of the American susceptibility to down-home hinterland values, and of the whimsical tone, even the self-mocking quality, of the American self-consciousness undergoing such psychic mobility.

One danger of misinterpreting instances from popular culture and from our politics is staying on the surface, of being hypnotized by externals, which function as recognition signals for regionalists as signs of their underlying non-urban values. Someone having some given characteristics is then favorably taken as "one of us." Sorokin was no more a simple provincial than Gandhi or Tolstoy. (And of course, neither was Mark Twain nor Will Rogers.) Sorokin appeared as a most distinguished outlander. Still there was one aspect familiar to regional Americans in his colorful rhetorical style, partly reminiscent of country-style "hell-fire-and-brimstone" preaching. It is obvious that even now anti-urban provincials carry this association over into secular politics. An old example was the rallying cry for Truman's whistle-stop campaign: "Give 'em hell, Harry!"

In no way do these illustrations claim that Sorokin, distant as he was from American thought and elitist as he saw himself in cultural matters, would have appealed to them himself. Let me go further; the ease of the American movement between hinterland and city typically reflects a loosely fitting and light-weight modernist overlay upon a profoundly regional spiritual core. Europe's historic divisions between gentry and peasantry, between central governments and provincials, go far deeper. As a result, such cleavages make their radial contrariety, as well as their vertical hierarchies, those between the urban wealthy and urban poor, much more serious. The New World's differences in this regard make for shallower cultural expressions, but also for much less *Angst* in its ambivalences. Americans take their politics more seriously than their films and television, but often with a notable degree of playfulness, circumstances permitting. One main point of this set of comparisons is to explore the attraction and relevance of Sorokin's views for Americans, and the degree to which Americans are likely to respond.

Let us see how the radial contrariety more deeply imbues American life than do the vertical vectors of social or economic power. Consider American political history. Radial polarities can be marked as obvious between: (1) colonies and home country; (2) Thomas Jefferson on the role of the yeoman farmer and on states' rights, as against Alexander Hamilton on sound currency and federal power; (3) Andrew Jackson as a hinterlander against Nicholas Biddle's National Bank; (but) (4) John Calhoun and the "nullifiers" versus President Jackson as executive of federal power; (5) the agrarian South versus the industrializing North in the American Civil War; (6) the contrasting styles and appeals of Populism and Progressivism; (7) the shift in the moral center of gravity during the Watergate hearings to two Southern senators, Sam Ervin and Howard Baker, both of whom incidentally had retained their regional values and pronounced accents.

A comment on the political aspect of the radial vector is appropriate here. At times an obviously regional leader takes over at the center; "Old Hickory" (Andrew Jackson), mentioned above, is a good example. Regionalism may be a positive factor in taking over or retaining power; for example, "Log Cabin and hard cider" electioneering themes, William McKinley's "front-porch" campaign, Harry Truman's "whistle-stop" race, California's grass-roots Proposition 13 against taxes, and so on. On the other hand, urbanites at the center become rather uneasy at the regional styles of Jackson, Lincoln, Truman, Lyndon Johnson, Jimmy Carter, or Bill Clinton.

Now, we may remark that the closing of the frontier at the end of the nineteenth century and the decline of the family farm in the twentieth in no way have eliminated regional values and self-consciousness which even now permeate American culture, whether political, literary, dramatic, or popular. More substantive than popular mass culture are the serious works of regional authors, such as Mark Twain, William Faulkner, John Steinbeck, William Saroyan, and Robert Penn Warren. In their works, far greater subtlety and complex mixtures of all sorts of contrarieties had been manifest, a prime example being Warren's *All the King's Men*, a classic treatment of human nature and populist politics loosely based upon the Huey Long story.

Although Sorokin was estranged from the optimistic and progressive side of the American psyche, and indeed from much of American culture, he appealed to the deep-seated reservations often held by Americans in their hinterlands moments about "city slickers" and urban corruption. Those in power or seeking it have often trimmed their sails to engage the strong sense of peripheralist wrath, as do politicians (however sincere in their regionalism) recently "running against the government." Carter, Reagan, Gephardt, and Gingrich are excellent present-day examples; in their own ways, and with quite varied success, they all sought to capture the winds of hinterlands outrage against the city. ("Throw the rascals out" seems to be of the same lineage as Jack Cade's "First we'll hang all the lawyers.")

Sorokin claims that three major "culture mentalities" in succession typify the modern age (1957, pp. 60ff.). The first, or positive, phase is marked by the "active sensate" attitude. This represents productivity and creative inventiveness, both in technology and in social innovations. Genuine achievements take place, and affirmative role models are then to be sought in urban centers. "Active sensate" leaders accordingly make up one down-to-earth sort of "creative minority" (Toynbee's term), setting forth ideals of worldly achievement.

The "passive sensate" mentality engages with the pursuit of pleasures, including those deemed "unnecessary" by Epicurus. In fact, it has to do with common denominator lures for urban idle rich and undeserving poor alike, and basically represents the simplest kind of lure for hinterlander customers and recruits. ("How you gonna keep 'em down on the farm, after they've seen Paree?" was the message of a World-War I song.) While "active sensate" enlistment points to things to be achieved, "passive sensate" values characterize things to be enjoyed, or good things to be had. During the whole "sensate" period, this intermediate phase represents a relative loss of creative impetus, a tendency to coast on one's oars.

The last, or "cynical sensate," stage is the extreme opposite of creativity, a falling into exploitation and corruption. One of its expressions would be complete defiance of accepted norms in the mindless pursuit of satisfactions. One of the features of decadence is invariably such gross self-display, typically magnified by the current media in advertising, entertainment, and news of celebrities. In our days, the aim of journalists and talk-show stars is the maximum attention paid to what they offer and the most profitable ratings. So they play both ends against the middle, flattering "free spirits" and disreputable types by publicizing them, and at the same time evoking the maximum moral indignation on the part of the respectable members of the audience by intimating their own shocked feelings.

Another obvious feature of the cynical sensate mentality is rather transparent hypocrisy, as in either the covering of one's own misdeeds, or the denouncing of misdeeds of rivals, in such exaggerated terms that the dullest hinterlander spots it as "phony." Uninhibited scramblings for the perquisites of wealth and power become intensified, as current crises turn the wheel of fortune faster and faster. Such hypocrisy plays up to, not so much the urban galleries, as the regional hinterlands. Urban hypocrisy is the tribute paid to the more old-fashioned regional virtue, which tends to be "idealistic" or "ideational." The distance from the usual urban style can make professed virtues ring false, as in uneasy alliances between opportunistic urban politicians and hinterlander "New Right" types. "Pseudoideational" phenomena often do go hand-in-hand with the cynical sensate, according to Sorokin's own classification (1957, pp. 51ff.).

While the active sensate stage appropriately celebrated as a role model someone like the Wizard of Menlo Park (Thomas Alva Edison), who actually did something, nowadays cynical sensate acclaim (for a time) goes to Wizards of Junk-Bonds (Michael Milken) and to other uncreative self-enriching promoters. (Consider typical book titles as illustrative of such thought: *The Art of the Deal, Making It, Winning through Intimidation, How to Swim with the Sharks, How to Profit from the Coming Crash, The Mayflower Madam*, etc.) In lieu of aristocrats, as essayist-journalist, Cleveland Amory, observed many years ago, we now have celebrities, persons famous for being famous; while the lurid lifestyles of the overpaid and notorious are matters of consuming, sometimes prurient, interest.

But many such symptoms may be only incidental, even when they outweigh comparable active sensate evidence, and, therefore, in terms of adverse images tend to undermine the moral authority of urban leaderships. Sorokin more often leveled his critique against serious breakdowns of standards than at superficial appearances, whether among the masses or within corrupt and tyrannical officialdom. The book he co-authored with Walter Lunden, *Power and Morality* (1959), emphasizes urban decay and misrule, following Lord Acton's dictum on the corruptions of power. At the present stage, one might hypothesize about conditions which magnify cynical sensate qualities of sociocultural phenomena. At any given time, technology heightens economic mechanisms generating "passive pleasures"; these still grind away. At pivotal points of leverage, great concentrations of wealth and prestige exist, but increasingly precariously, since conditions threaten severe crises to come. The atmosphere among elites becomes that of *"Après moi le déluge,"* or "Take the money and run." Corruption among traders, savings and loan managers, brokerage firms, TV evangelists, Housing and Urban Development officials, politicians, television personalities, etc., are heightened by calculations that opportunities to steal or swindle or deal or delude might suddenly dry up.

Under rapid changes, central urban hierarchies are more and more unstable, while struggles increase among speculators and politicians contending for the levers of power. If anticipation of crises necessarily mark the late sensate age, then "cynical sensate" phenomena should invariably appear, with all prestige, wealth, and power becoming highly perishable commodities. Consequently, hinterlands or ethnic neighborhoods that identify with the distant, but non-urban, values of the "old country" (You can take the immigrant out of the old country, but you can't take the old country out of the immigrant) are far less tightly bound symbiotically to Cosmopolis with all its temptations and corruptions.

3. Sagecraft

More needs saying on sages, to throw light on the inner dynamics of the radial contrariety and to compare sages of different backgrounds.

A society's values are best presented by its sages. Artists often shape their details and suggest their ambiance, but while artists are sometimes sages (Mark Twain or Leo Tolstoy), the sage *per se* properly conveys the value content of the culture.

Earlier, we remarked that Tolstoy and Sorokin are more than popular philosophers, they are sages. Which Americans deserve that title? Our national self-consciousness can well be recognized in the works and writing of Benjamin Franklin, Ralph Waldo Emerson, Mark Twain, and Will Rogers. All four illustrate complexities in the role of sage to which attention should be drawn.

One complexity is this: the sage, however regional he may be, does not simply iterate folk-wisdom. For this, our grandsires are sufficient. Sages, classical or modern, engage with live issues impacting both the City and its hinterlands. (For instance, the classical sage Lao-tse commented upon bureaucratic governance.)

Benjamin Franklin played a dual part in his "Poor Richard" or regional and colonial image and in his creative leadership in Philadelphia's urban affairs. The French were enchanted with his simple fur-hatted persona, as a Rouseauistic colonial outlander. But he also stood at the center of American power center developments, so here was a marked urban/regional polarity within Franklin, as well as a timeliness to his sagely contributions.

The second sage, Emerson, had a lengthy career throughout much of the nineteenth century. In such writings as "The American Scholar," "Nature," "Self-Reliance," and "The Divinity School Address," he set forth distinctive American insights and values, outlandish to the old European power centers. The occasions for his work were, like Tolstoy's, quite contemporary and vital. A general conclusion follows regarding sages; they draw liberally upon broad cultural resources shared by the City and the hinterlands in the consideration of significant questions for emerging modernity. The literary giant Mark Twain, erstwhile riverboat pilot and frontier journalist, is our third exemplary sage. Like Emerson, he commented forcefully upon slavery, and like a fourth sage, Will Rogers, with whom he had otherwise much in common, he made incisive remarks upon national governing institutions. It is unnecessary to say more about Mark Twain.

The case of Will Rogers is different, since his writings were fewer and of a more ephemeral quality. Like Twain, he was a speaker of deceptively subtle power, with acutely relevant and humane sentiments. His untimely death in an airplane crash, along with the pioneer aviator Wiley Post, deprived America, during our dismal Depression years, of much-needed wisdom and morale-building. (I am old enough to remember *and* believe that this was America's greatest individual loss since Lincoln's assassination.) The dynamics of the radial contrariety played themselves out most obviously with Twain and Rogers, less apparently with Emerson, and interestingly with Franklin.

Given my professed bias in favor of regionalists, do I imply that "urban sage" is a contradiction in terms? Not necessarily. One could call Socrates, Dr. Samuel Johnson, Raymond Aron, Walter Lippmann, Reinhold Niebuhr and even Mortimer Adler "urban sages." However, one qualifying point must be made. City intellectuals frequently oscillate on shallow ideological coordinates, pundits and journalists chase the bottom line and deadlines. Urban sages reach far back for their values, and much they say resonates well in the provinces, where wisdom is also deeply rooted. Consider Niebuhr's critique of power centers and "collective egoisms"; the hinterlanders fervantly agree with Lord Acton's and Niebuhr's suspicion of power.

4. Dissatisfaction with Sorokin's Critique

Upon the radial contrariety distinguishing the poles of pro-urban and pro-regional values, one should place Talcott Parsons toward one side and Pitirim A. Sorokin toward the other. Their positions are by no means mutually exclusive in every respect. Sorokin himself discerned common ground between Parsons's *The Social System* (1951) and his own *Society, Culture, and Personality* (1947), in his "Similarities and Dissimilarities," *Fads and Foibles* (1956), and in the more magisterial *Sociological Theories of Today* (1966). Two accountings might be given regarding their relatively unnoticed parallels. One would be that Parsons's concurrence with so many of Sorokin's ideas was largely unconscious, or that it reflected points that he took as already established "common coin" in the profession. Another reading would be that Parsons, having explored the implications of interrelated mainline ideas, was simply unfolding what was implicit in a theory compounded from major social thinkers. Which of these readings is correct is less important than the way the shared ground between Parsons and Sorokin constitutes a set of agreements that excludes follies typical of the age. Their common ground stands firm despite the other gaps, or even chasms, between the two men.

More elucidation is needed at this point. The basic content of the Parsons-Sorokin overlap finds its summary statement on pages 420 through 431 of Sorokin's *Sociological Theories of Today* under the following rubrics: "Meaningful Interaction as the Basic Process"; "Trinity of Personality, Society, and Culture"; "Three Forms of Meaningful Culture Patterns"; "The Concept of System"; "Cultural System"; "Social System and its Properties"; "Change in Social Systems"; and "Personality System." Those headings cover the reminiscent themes advanced by both scholars, which all have to do with sociocultural values.

To this one can add two value-related points. From their different angles, Sorokin and Parsons each deeply appreciated the thought of Alfred North Whitehead. Sorokin admired the Platonic elements in Whitehead, while Parsons found Whitehead's emphasis on the need for scientific theory a great stimulus. Secondly, both men had deep doubts about classical liberal economics, and about Utilitarianism and Marxism. In short, neither could be said to be narrowly empiricistic nor, indeed in any sense, simply fashionably ideological. Their relative immunity to charges of scientistic shallowness follows from their sociocultural affirmations which inspire their respective civilizational studies, but less so their profoundly different evaluations of modernity.

Parsons and Sorokin had very different purposes which threw into shadow their common ground. The "grand theory" of Parsons hopefully approximated an emerging consensual approach to problems of economics and administration. His "structural-functionalism," as it was labelled, was an appeal to urban professionals of great power and influence. The theorists, and the wider audiences, addressed by each scholar were very different. Parsons would be preferred by the academic establishment to one whose doubts about the "sensate culture" were so profound. The ambitions and the interests their thinking carried, the audiences addressed, and the historic origins of their positions diverged too greatly. Complementarity is the best to be hoped for with regard to fundamentally contrasting upbeat and downbeat readings of modernity.

Their works attracted the allegiance of different reference groups, yet they each pull together materials in their own domains, drawing upon ranges of agreement. Beyond this, they give rational guidance. In each case, what kind of heuristics do we have? Deeper examination reveals that these are heuristics not just for inquiry, though they incorporate scientific methods, but for the assemblage of facts and values. In short, they serve as frameworks for interpretation, encasements for thought, as structural scaffoldings within which both data and norms can be arranged. In these frameworks, "public philosophies" are developed for the use of two sorts of educated citizens. One group has primarily administrative interests, while the other attempts the long view of human history. Both trends, broadly based socially and taken as heuristics of assemblage for facts and values, jointly contribute to what may fairly be called the "Big Picture."

What are the chief differences between Sorokin and Parsons? Parsons took a temporally short range, but very broad-gauged outlook upon modernity. He provided an ethos and rationale for the administrator of cosmopolitan institutions and for his scientific advisers, among them the professional sociologists. Much of his work carries the explanatory positions, the self-image and the total outlook, going along with the bedside manner of mandarins for modernity. Where Confucius drew upon literary classics and social custom, Parsons drew upon growing social sciences, all construed as somehow unitary and as underlying the learned and skilled professions across the range of their interlocking tasks. In brief, one notices the built-in rational progressivism in Parsons's outlook.

In contrast, Sorokin's philosophy of history warned about the vulnerability of human institutions, those which Parsons tended to treat as secure and safe. The senior scholar took a long view showing the clay feet of Cosmopolis. He stands back from a great distance, while Parsons and Parsonians identify with professionals and administrators. Parsonian scholars, like Arthur Miller's Willy Loman, go forth with a smile and a shoeshine, and perhaps with chewing gum and bailing wire, to keep our secular institutions going, but not in Sorokinian ashes and sackcloth.

The susceptibility of human organizations to decay was underlined by Sorokin, since his hinterland point of view embraced a far longer span than did that of the more urban Parsons. But the common ground between Parsons and Sorokin, acknowledged grudgingly by Sorokin himself, is neutral territory lying halfway between the two rival grand theories, sheltered from the rumbling crossfire of controversy. In the contest, Parsons comes across as the spokesman for Cosmopolis, for what David Wilkinson has called "Central Civilization" (Melko and Scott 1987). Sorokin demonstrated more provincial and peripheral values, reacting against modern centers of power and influence. Accordingly, he pointed to vulnerabilities and dangers of the modern world. His attacks upon "sensate" culture in its "overripeness" document his suspicion that urban establishmentarians do not always deserve to be trusted, given the ill consequences of so many even well-intended ventures and practices. (Consider Vietnam,

Afghanistan, the Soviet collapse, the American debt, the United States involvements in Somalia and Bosnia.)

With all this controversial cannonading, we find two adversarial perspectives on modernity, the cleavage between which reflected the intellectual politics of an era. Sorokin was addressing, we might say preaching to, a broader and less academically specialized audience consisting of deeply skeptical provincials and outsiders, to whom the City's golden promises of progress had less validity. On their positive side, a quasi-mythic aura attends Sorokin's ideas, especially those values associated with the ideational and the idealistic cultures. However, Parsons's and Sorokin's rival modes of sagacity, each in its way, serve as frames for symbolic adjustive processes accommodating data and norms. Both, to follow Sorokin's phrase, are "continuous in a sense" with science (Anderle 1965, p. 54). Their larger views, or promotional prospectuses, are not simply the same as science in either case. So they would say of one another, however unappreciatively, and so other critics of them both do suggest, also unfavorably. (Think of Robert Merton, Robert Bierstadt, and George Homans.) These enframements hold steady two contrasting readings of today's sociocultural realm, the City insider's and the peripheral outsider's.

Parsons stood more or less as a qualified optimist, while Sorokin's views have been scorned by urban sociologists and political scientists as unduly "pessimistic," even though Sorokin affirmed chances for new values arising from the collapse of the sensate system. Another basic contrast is this: Parsons should be regarded as a serious bourgeois, while those city types classified by Sorokin as "passive sensate" and "cynical sensate" are decidedly shallow, rather than serious. Parsons focuses on durable structural elements in a society less immediately subject to decline and decay, whereas Sorokin finds many features of our world taking us the way of Tyre and Sidon. Are not both these sorts of aspects fairly open and obvious? Anyone with normal capacity for taking notice can recognize them. The City puts its best foot forward for Parsons, its worst for Sorokin. Between Parsons and Sorokin, the whole range of phenomena would seem to be fully described, whether hale or sickly.

How, then, does one sum up the contrast? How is justice to be done between their accounts? Talcott Parsons, and in great part with good reason, presented a far rosier view of modernity than did Sorokin. While Sorokin observed, as through an outlander/hinterlander's disapproving eyes, the teeterings of loosely-joined urban hierarchies, in all their corrupt actuality, Parsons, as a rational liberal and as an insider, saw the hierarchies as ideally interrelated, grounded scientifically, and administered by skilled service-oriented professionals. He, in effect, spoke on behalf of idealized role models alluded to in public life, and, incidentally, dramatized in urban-influenced popular culture. (Films and television dramas focusing upon professionals within cities often idealize their heroes.)

While Sorokin had described the manifest naughtinesses, greed, and violence of our world, Parsons projected an ideal meritocratic system, where professionals are truly in touch with science, with one another, and are listened to by responsible wielders of large-scale "social action." And as Confucius well knew, there is the rub, persuading the princes of this world, the presidential appointees and their like, to take good advice. But the basic truth in Parsons's portrayal of the modern world lies in the dedication of those professional good guys who, unlike the cynical types, do not seek the spotlight but, despite crises, do their duty. Sorokin's and Parsons's two tales of the City are both true in their own way.

5. The Complexity of Contrarieties

Physical mobility we know about; it is basic to social physics as pursued by our civilizationist colleagues Arthur Iberall and David Wilkinson. Social mobility we have been told about by Sorokin and later thinkers. Psychic mobility is implied by Sorokin's treatment of internalizing norms and shifts among projected values, and it is implied by free movement expressed in conversions and re-orientations generally. Consider the sayings, "You can take the boy out of the country, but you can't take the country out of the boy," and "You can't go home again." Both proverbs allude to limiting constraints on the psychic mobility which would otherwise allow the taking on of new values.

The picturing of value-contrasting contrarieties as vectors allows us to contemplate polar differences in opposition, that is, where one or the other side is favored, or where both are objects of satire or humor—as in much popular culture—or where there is considered a change in values, a psychic movement away from one pole toward the other.

Radial contrarieties may be of greater or lesser range. One of these can be labelled "rurbification," as by Sorokin and Zimmermann, with its two poles being rural and urban, where the psychic (as well as actual) interplay between the two gives rise to cultural syntheses. A broader, more relevant version, given the decline of purely rural influences, is that between urban centers and peripheral regions or provinces. A third, more extended radius yet, is that between superpowers and their outlands. This one may plausibly be titled "Westernization."

Now, at the outer pole of these radii, regional spokespersons and leaders consciously strive against the secularity of their urban opposites by emphasizing traditional religion, simplicity, primary relationships, informality, and local historic roles. Urban centers, given the greater concentration of wealth and power, display far more prominent vertical vectors, social, economic, and political. Regional leaders strategically de-emphasize their own local hierarchies by mobilizing values shared with their followers against oppressive, sometimes impious, "city slickers."

Vertical lines represent other contrarieties; these are to be found, though they are less apparent, in places other than the city. But urban communications make those contrasts widely resonate: capitalists and managers as opposed to workers; social leaders as opposed to the excluded; empowered elders as against youth; Philistine and conventional art establishments as against Bohemians. In late sensate eras, convulsive pressures from below heighten the confusion, sometimes giving rebel voices from hinterlands or even outlands increased moral authority.

We can envisage most of today's dynamic contrarieties including the rural-urban vector. The rural-urban vector is radial in nature, rather than hierarchical, as are those social, economic, and political vectors of most concern to urban thinkers. All these vectors, including the radial one, serve as tracking routes for psychic mobility, for shiftings in values. They suggest that value patterns in the world are very much conditioned adversarially, one's psychic position being set in contrast to where it is not. As a negative example in the adversarial mode, urban snobbery and regional moral superiority alike operate on that radial vector laid out between backwater and urban cesspool. In contrast, symbiosis allows for positive identifications in both directions; we can construe appropriate psychic mobility as an often sympathetic oscillation within a certain range on the polar radial vector.

Built-in difficulties that come with this horizontal and vertical vectoral model demand elucidation. What are the workings of these spatial metaphors? The horizontal, non-hierarchical vector resembles the vertical ones in the simple respect of being determined by opposite or polar values. Going to the heart of the matter, while ignoring all complications, one can say that "distance" represents "differences" between values or perspectives.

One difference which has importance is the way radial vectors, unlike vertical ones, resist being hierarchized. Now, hinterlanders and outlanders may give *de facto* recognition to the power of "the city," but they resist acknowledgement of its authority, whether *de facto* or *de jure*. Urban subordinates may grudgingly recognize the *de facto* authorities, even while rebelling against them. For their part, hinterlanders tend to defer only to hinterland magnates and leaders, who shrewdly undertake to flatten out their own status and affirm against Cosmopolis the simple values they share with their humbler neighbors. Much of American culture and politics throws light on this contrast. The special role of Congress and the state primaries—where "country slickers" of Iowa and New Hampshire take urbanite journalists and politicos for their quadrennial rides—can be taken as typical. The contrast should be generalized further, though in other cultures the regional-urban radial vector can be less conspicuous. The vertical social vector seems more basic, for example, to the class-riddled culture of Great Britain.

Two built-in difficulties for the model, perhaps for political historians the over-riding ones, are, first, "big-frog-in-small-pond" phenomena; that is, the insistence of regional gentry upon their local privileges, however modest when contrasted with urban "big-frog-in-large-pond" status. Secondly, the most riveting contrariety for realists would arise when a power center is challenged for dominance by a rival. Here the question arises as to *which* point is to be the center of radiating power. All history is rife with such great contentions and biddings for world leadership. The challengers, like bull sea lions advancing upon some reigning beachmaster, seek to make the maximum impression. They do not approach with foxy regional humility, but with pomp and all banners flying. Hitler went in for pretentious display in the Nuremberg rallies, and he found Wilhelmine architecture much too modest. The Chancery had to be brought to grandiosity by Albert Speer, and one of Hitler's last inquiries was "Is Paris burning?" This does throw light upon such phenomena as the so–called "edifice complex" of politicians, Bellah's "civil religion," and Veblen's "conspicuous consumption." Such displays are made to overawe one's own hinterlanders, and to intimidate possible rivals.

What is the answer? Our model can handle most contrarieties, but not purely localized, petty hierarchical vanities, and not the great efforts to shift the power center itself. The "rurbification" or "Westernization" vector is internal to a power system as between a center and its peripheries. Its dialectic can involve different players with much different strategies: highly-placed holders of power as against apparently weaker, but subtler, hinterland or outland leaders. (One interesting complication is the way the central power may and often must recruit regional talent to take over at the center to save itself from internal incompetence.)

The aspects of the active and overripe sensate stages recounted by Sorokin fit reasonably well into this latter polarity, whereas great power struggles must be read, in the spirit of Thucydides and of Toynbee, as tragic civil contentions within a civilization and as relative breakdowns of rationality. Sorokin and Toynbee discovered that they had a lot in common during their exchanges at Salzburg. Practically speaking, many of their views ran parallel, despite the fact that Sorokin was more deeply marked by the hinterland than was Toynbee.

Capitalism and socialism serve as rallying cries, clashing pronouncements on what should be in terms of highly urban readings of the politico-economic vector. In these ideologies, the regionalist factor is left out of account; hinterlanders are seen as only recruits-to-be for the mills, and Karl Marx himself spoke of the "idiocy of rural life." Yet, the answer to the social scientist Werner Sombart's shrewd question as to why America so strongly resists socialism lies in the force of radial vectors in this country, forbidding any cut-and-dried, purely urban solution. Sorokin's views most impertinently reinforced this peripheral resistance, heightening the aggravation of urban advisory groups soliciting "hearts and minds" from hinterlands and outlands alike. By his challenge to modernity, he undermines the respect sought by dominant urban figures attempting to recruit, lead, and, at their best, professionalize the hinterlanders. This, in my judgment, accounts for savagely reactive counter-critiques of Sorokin.

Along the vertical vectors, much takes place as authorities press down from above and hitherto dominated groups contend vigorously from beneath; the social and political-economic contrarieties of the power centers are the most conspicuous in arousing adversarial tensions from below. Picture Groucho Marx ridiculing grande dames and opera impresarios, while Karl Marx was in full revolt against the hated bourgeoisie; American, French, German, and recently Chinese youth demonstrating against their elders; modern artists against establishments of the city and artists of the hinterlands. Sometimes, a snobbish urban journal such as *Partisan Review* combined the Marxist, Freudian, and aesthetic revolts. Urban satirists would weigh in with sly comments and mischievous pranks, such as the journalist's placing a midget on John Pierpoint Morgan's knee during a Congressional hearing. These would sell both in the city and in the hinterlands, as confirming de-legitimations of presumed authorities, to the delight of both urban underdogs and of regionalists.

Cosmopolis is usually too self-absorbed to recognize the very non-hierarchical adversarial dynamic present in the radial vector. Those who come forth to speak for the hinterlands and outlands, their regional magnates and leaders, make a virtue of necessity, as local hierarchies are less steep than those of the court of Versailles, of bureaucracies, or of mega–corporations. Spokespersons emphasize informality, family and personal relationships, also religious and community ties. The wily Senator Sam Ervin was just a "simple country lawyer," Will Rogers claimed he only knew "what he read in the papers," Leo Tolstoy conspicuously wore a peasant's smock; and Mohandas Gandhi, a simple dhoti. All of this remarkable jujitsu turned the pomp and circumstance, the "colossalism" and "conspicuous consumption," of the city against itself, and gave fellow hinterlanders their sense of having allies. Hinterlanders certainly depend less upon the pompous and the impersonal for their recognition signals. Sorokin, like Tolstoy, proclaimed the value of the idealistic, the ideational, and the altruistic against the most obvious traits of City in decline. With such affirmations, further depreciations of urban monumentality and lavish accoutrements are inevitable. Regional magnates often appeal to their personal status, quite apart from external signs of pomp, "Where MacTavish sits, there is the head of the table," or to widely shared communal pieties.

So far, we have examined Sorokin's dialectical assault upon modernity, where it came from, and what it comes to. Its basic feature is the way it illustrates the polar tensions displayed between value systems of modernity and those of hinterlands and outlands (including heirs of other civilizations), values of the core and its immediate and distant peripheries. Sorokin's strong critique of the "overripe sensate" culture awakened sympathy among opponents of Westernization. Current tensions are destined to produce many such bipolar urban-regional vectoral relations, along with their anti-urban affinities shared not only among regions, but also in distantly impacted outlands. Sorokin himself dramatized those tensions in his own person. Yet such tensions call for reconciliation. Consider the following chart.

CORRELATED LIFE PATTERNS

SCALE	CORRELATIONS	IN SOCIAL SCIENCES	IN THE ARTS
Massive	With vast systematic interactions. A high-level scanning of overall "traffic patterns," with too much distance for the human. Roles are seen as causal linkages within larger systems.	"Social physics," the study of impersonal systems, such as geopolitics, *Realpolitik*, or market analysis.	Where the self is swamped as an atom. Kafka; Chaplin's *Modern Times;* Lang's *Metropolis;* much modern architecture; non-representational painting, such as Pollock's; "Pop Art" like Warhol's; Theater of the Absurd.
Mid-scale or Personal	With patterns that can be commended as apt or worthwhile. Exemplifications that *may* also be seen as exemplary, "Worldviews" included. The role grasped in its integrity is conveyed through emulation.	Studies involving sociocultural "meanings," susceptible to *Verstehen* or the "logico-meaningful method." Shared ground between Weber, Sorokin, and Parsons. This level joins the humanities and sciences.	*Poesis,* such as philosophical poetry; most novels and drama; representative art displaying character and humanly meaningful contexts, such as Rembrandt, George Catlin, Norman Rockwell.
Minute	With fragmentary, privatized moments and moods. Its microscopic closeness allows too little distance for the human.	Associationism; psychological hedonism; Freudianism; Behaviorism (such as dealings with ideas, wants and impulses, stimuli and responses).	Where the self is pulverized. Impressionism; Expressionism; Surrealism; short lyrics of momentary mood; "stream of consciousness" writing.

What sort of reconciliation can be sought despite the radial contrariety? As a visual aid to reconciling the regionalist and the urban administrator, also the macrosociologist Sorokin and the structural-functionalist Parsons, we employ the preceding chart, the heart and center of which displays their common ground. That diagram throws light on Sorokin's and Parsons's joint virtues, in contrast to social and methodological theories repugnant to both.

The three scales–massive, midscale, and minute–refer to perspectives taken upon patterns discernible in human affairs. The midscale reference is central (the others being definable in its terms), and it apprehends patterns capable of being chosen and modified by the individual, hence capable of commendation. Norms and roles are at issue here. The massive viewing is that of patterns of interrelated patterns; such complex characters themselves being incapable of being chosen. The minute patterns are also not to be chosen. These are the regularities which underlie or condition choice but cannot constitute it. The covering law approach holds sway over the massive, be it economic or geopolitical, and the minute, be it behaviorist or Freudian. By contrast, the mid-scale range is consistent with the descriptive dimension, stressed by the positivists, and the normative dimension which is appropriate for the proponents of *Verstehen*. Parsons, while as an economist, frequently scanning the massive range, finds, as a rational liberal, his midscale center of gravity in professional normatives, or in responsible roles. Confucius's thought, interestingly enough, throws up a fine bridge between Parsons and Sorokin. Sorokin's emphasis upon the centrality of norms for personalities and social groups needs no documentation. In short, the double aspect of the midscale, that is, the factuality of its regular patterns and their potential for being regulative through approbative emulation, establishes within its scope the best juncture between humanities and human sciences. Perspectival renderings, and shifts among these, allow escape from any and all claims that social science entails nihilism.

Cosmopolis does foster massive and minute approaches to social reflection, and this disposition within urban sociology accentuated differences with Sorokin, given his more peripheral stance and sympathies. Yet, the needs for administrative oversight of the massive, and attention to motivational factors for the exercise of leadership, do not preclude responsibility. Quite the contrary. Parsons, on the secular "calling" of the urban professional, retains a midscale orientation, as does Sorokin with his integralism. So both scholars hold the fort against reductive positivism.

In summary, three scales allow for our attending to human affairs–the massive, the mid-scale, and the minute. At those points where Parsons faithfully followed up on themes from Max Weber, who emphasized *Verstehen*, and where Sorokin articulated the "logico-meaningful method," both men steered between extremes. One extreme was the massive perspective in which roles are seen not as valuable emulative patterns, but rather in relation to other roles in a total system, and its opposite was the minute, pulverizing scale apt for looking at psychological stimuli and responses or Freudian drives. Modernity encourages the high-altitude viewing where all roles fall into a large pattern of patterns, where individual persons become intermediate linkages in a vaster structure. The saving virtue shared by Sorokin and Parsons is that they managed to preserve the human, in ways in which behaviorism, sociobiology, neo-Marxism and neo-conservatism do not.

The complementarity of Parsons and Sorokin illustrated in this account should be appreciated. Parsons is neither to be construed as an ideologue (Jeffrey Alexander faithfully and well made this point [1983, p. 294]), nor as an institutional conformist (Edward Shils referred to "miscreants" who misrepresented Parsons [1980, p. 192]). Secondly, Sorokin's sophistication and breadth of learning must be allowed to outweigh modernist snobbery against traditional values standing as "live options," but ensconced nowadays more obviously in the provinces and outlands than in Cosmopolis. Those who paid respectful attention to Sorokin tended to identify wholeheartedly with provinces and territories not yet fully assimilated to the urban West, in general, nor the big City, in particular. The pluralism of values implied by Sorokin's oscillation theory allows for much needed shifts to provincially based affiliations. Such shifts have come to be roughly reintroduced by the rough dialectic of history. Regarding such crisis points, Sorokin's dealing with "familistic" values, and with "polarization" resulting from critical impacts, can be quite illuminating.

Alfred North Whitehead, appreciated by both Sorokin and Parsons, once observed that Western thought is a "series of footnotes to Plato." The Platonism marking Sorokin's "integralism" is manifest. Less directly Platonic is Parsons's rational liberalism, but like the thought of Locke, Kant, Weber, Jaspers, and more locally at Harvard, C. I. Lewis and John Rawls, it does have its remote ancestry in Plato's rational authoritarianism, where the culturative projection of the Forms (patterns for emulation) gives structure to human efforts. More effectively than Plato, the rational liberals make their contrarieties symbiotic rather than adversarial. Plato had to resort to Transcendence for providing the grounding to principles, and the "noble lie" for providing the guardians' justifications in practice. Parsons's administrators, by contrast, are liberalized guardians being guided by scientific truth *in lieu* of visionary forms and ideally seeking justification by both ideals and expertise. Sorokin's position has older visionary qualities, still found alive and well upon the civilizational peripheries.

Now we reach the conclusion that Sorokin, from the periphery, and Parsons, from the cosmopolitan center, not only have some shared assumptions but usefully complementary modes of wisdom, even when to all appearances, they are most unalike. "Public philosophy" can well draw upon both contrasting sets of insights.

6. Civilizational Implications

Now, all the distinctive characteristics of Sorokin's work, particularly those most looked at askance by urban critics, bring rich advantages to comparative civilizational scholarship. Consider, first of all, the breadth of his perspective. Like Oswald Spengler, but in terms of scholarly responsibility more close to Toynbee, Sorokin gathered together reams of data in civilizational research in his *Social and Cultural Dynamics*. All three of these thinkers, whatever the differences among them, spelled out in Sorokin's own *Social Philosophies in an Age of Crisis* and *Sociological Theories of Today,* tended to jolt readers out of Western monocentrism. Wider viewings of our world should have been sought by scholars and general readers in any case, given the rough course of the twentieth century. That Spengler, Toynbee, and Sorokin are often spoken of together, even when in dismissal, reflects the shock they had given to European-centered complacency among the learned. (In one sense, William McNeill's *Rise of the West* [1963] is a sophisticated riposte to them, as Paul Kennedy's *Rise and Fall of the Great Powers* [1987] stands as a qualified confirmation.)

The features Sorokin shares with other such macrosociological thinkers and visionary philosophers of history and culture had been set out by him in the two previous sources and summed up in the Salzburg proceedings, *Problems of Civilization*.

> The first basic agreement of these theories is: that in the boundless ocean of socio-cultural phenomena there

exist vast cultural entities—your "intelligible fields of study" or cultural super-systems or civilizations, which live and function as a real unity. It is not identical with the state or the nation or any other social group. The second important agreement with respect to the vastest cultural entities is that their total number in the whole history of human culture is very small: nine, ten, twenty-one "civilizations"; or, according to the different approach, two or three or five main types of cultural super-systems, the total number of these main types is comparatively very small. The third point of agreement is that each of these basic types of cultural prototypes is different from the others. The chief difference is that each of the vast cultural systems or civilizations is based upon some major premise or philosophical presupposition, or in the terminology of Spengler: prime symbol, which the super-systems or civilizations articulate, realizes in all its main compartments or parts in the process of its life career. Correspondingly, each of the great cultural unities is either logically or aesthetically consistent in the meaningful aspect of its part of compartments. The fifth concordance is that each of these super-systems, grounded in empirical reality, is a meaningful—causal or holistic unity. The sixth point of agreement concerns the general characteristics of the super-systems or civilizations, namely: its reality, which is different from that of its parts; its general and differential conductivity, dependence of its parts upon one another, upon the whole and of the whole upon its parts; preservation of its individuality of its sameness, despite a change of its parts; change in togetherness, immanent change and self determination of its life career, with external forces, either accelerating or slowing up, facilitating or hindering, the unfolding of the potentialities of the super-system or civilization, sometimes even destroying it; the selectivity of the super-system or civilization,

> accepting what is congenial to it and rejecting what is uncongenial; finally, the limited variability of the super-systems of civilization. There are other less important points of similarity but I want to stress at this moment that, in spite of quite different approaches and premisses which we have as investigators of these problems, in spite of these differences, we can and do arrive at a number of basic points of agreement in the study of civilizations or cultural systems and super-systems. (Anderle 1964, pp. 55-56)

The difficulties such an ambitious summation can cause for behaviorists, positivists, and other nominalists are daunting, if not insuperable. Yet, I think that some such principles as Sorokin draws up are essential for cultural studies when these range widely and call for an adequate accounting in social terms. The close interplay between culture and society, especially under conditions of massive trends carried into crisis, emerges sharply in Sorokin's work, and particularly with his "law of polarization."

In my earlier chapter, "Sorokin versus American Thought," I considered whether his "supersystems" might not be more properly read as *modi vivendi* among lesser systems rather than as he put the matter in his somewhat sweeping Platonic style (Talbutt 1980). Nonetheless, I once more raise the question of what kind of reality may be fairly imputed to "ideational," "idealistic," and "sensate" supersystems. What are they really? First, I am now inclined to take them as sociocultural, more particularly as axiological, functions. (William James took consciousness as a function; it did not thereby lack reality.) Let me add this: the relative predominances of Sorokin's "supersystems" resemble socioaxiological phasal aspects of the Spenglerian and Toynbeean civilizations, which themselves constitute unique "concrete universals." Sorokin's supersystems peak at certain points and are thus more "real" then than elsewhen.

This argument would no doubt be unsettling to nominalists, but, typically, most persons who operate under some "supersystem" or other proceed just as if it were a valid guiding framework. Even non-conformists recognize the force of institutions enacted through their contemporaries' doings. One such individual in some era could be cautious so as not to be burned at the stake for heresy; another at another time would not be greatly surprised at receiving pornographic ads in the mail or on his computer. Axiological trends working themselves out factually do seem to legitimate the "supersystem" as a guiding predictive device followed in one spirit by its adherents, and more weakly by reluctant contemporaries, and in another, yet analogous, interpretive way by an historical macrosociologist. The supersystem gets its ideal status from being contemplatable in its dominant phase and its concrete actuality through being made manifest by human agency. That duality allows for the crucial two-sided "meaningful causal" aspects of social phenomena, upon which Sorokin so rightly insists.

One advantage of an abstract sociocultural entity having such scope—as in its dominating a phasal aspect of a civilization—lies in its generality, its repeatable appearance at various times, and its ability to characterize concrete universals. This scope and range offers the comparativist a framework yielding lines of inquiry as to how far certain features do or do not appear. Furthermore, "ideational" and "idealistic" themes are neither so central nor prestigious in today's industrialized West as they have been and are in other parts of the world. So Sorokin's orientation allows for readier imaginative reach into Mideastern, south Asian, and east Asian cultures, for example, than does that of Enlightenment progressivism.

Still, progressivism, as Comtean thought, early on exerted a major influence upon Sorokin. Sorokin's theory of cultural oscillations I still read as a Platonizing of Comte's law of three stages, reversing its valorization by affirming the worth of the theological and metaphysical phases, thus turning unidirectionality into "rhythms" rather than into cycles—since the "idealist" supersystem does not inevitably appear. That interpretation satisfies me, if not Jaworski; perhaps it can be enriched by the radial contrariety notion (see Jaworski 1993). Sorokin temporalizes the erstwhile "spatial" hinterland/outland power center vector. This temporalization takes place in virtue of the way those "out in the sticks" tend, other things being equal, to be "behind the times." The farther out, the greater the "cultural lag" seems to become. (But contrariwise, often the *avant-garde* strikes the hinterlander as having "backslided" from any acceptable moral standards; so not all such worldly changes count as progress. The drumbeats of the 1994 and 1996 elections suggest as much.)

That incorporative move by Sorokin has justification since civilizations can best be taken as center-plus-hinterlands, their scope plausibly including "spheres of influence." The differential values, or axiological imbalance, between peripheries and center yield a powerful interactive dynamic. When the momentum from the radial contrariety becomes heavy enough, sociocultural crises manifest themselves. The immanent causation of the supersystems, or their presumed "dialectic," can also be reinforced by outlands-based tensions. Sorokin's "principle of limits" could profitably be read in some such terms.

The discussion begins to approach a focus. That is to say that the distinctiveness of Sorokin appears as a particularly strong, and tremendously well-informed, expression of radial contrariety drawn from the peripheral angle of vision. Americans themselves take a more symbiotic, less adversarial stance toward dominant power centers, even when, as usually happens, the radial contrariety more deeply imbues their attitudes than do urban-based social and economic vectors. (This holds despite the continual focusing by national, and consequently urban-based, media upon the latter sorts.) The "rurbification" interplay continues on past the rural versus the urban contrast to that of regions versus national power centers.

Where is Cosmopolis, really? Recently, communications and movement have greatly diffused the centers which had always been on the move in any event; Madison Avenue, Wall Street, the Chicago futures markets, Hollywood or "Tinsel-Town," major corporate headquarters of the Fortune 500, "inside the Beltway," and where else? Certainly not in the provinces. But today we Americans worry somewhat about the rise of the Ginza and of Zurich, among other international aspects of an increasingly diffuse Cosmopolitan "center" that is drifting out of the control of earlier power brokers.

Sorokin gave favorable readings of Eastern worldviews and civilizational values, especially favorably noting their aptness for Ideational and Idealistic classification in his *Social and Cultural Dynamics*. Although he had drawn most of the data from the Western tradition, his sympathies were such that he intensely pursued analogies with south Asian and east Asian cultures. Background for this appreciation lies in the thought of Tolstoy, who had been officially denounced for heresy by Orthodox authorities. Some aspects of this are highly ironic; Tolstoy was in great part shaped by the Enlightenment in his de-emphasis upon traditional Christian doctrines, though also in part by mystical Slavophilism. In fact, Tolstoy's generalized mysticism made him—and consequently Sorokin as well—more available to Easterners, to whom Christology and soteriology would have been quite alien. That transmissibility is attested to by Professor

Hallen's article giving tribute to Sorokin as most relevant to Indian thought in *Sorokin and Sociology* (Hallen and Prajad 1972). That is one instance of the sympathetic reverberations awakened by Sorokin on the inner and outer peripheries of "Central Civilization." Another clue to the attraction Sorokin's thought holds for outlanders is the impressive number of translations made of his writings.

Finally, "Westernization," like "rurbification," is a bipolar interaction, with something going on at both poles. It is not a simple spreading of Cosmopolis out into the sticks, nor just a conveying of advanced technology to those who sit in darkness. Today's world is so much afflicted by mutual jostling that no civilization can exist in pristine isolation. Shangri-La has totally vanished. So, comparative civilizational studies must reach far back in time to find pure insulated cases. Under the conditions of modernity, everyone suffers from the "Messerschmitt twitch"—not just about war (and politics), but threatened cultural values as well. Sorokin's outland/hinterland stance concerning "overripe sensate" phenomena indicates the type of reactive response Westernization everywhere elicits. His chief relevance to civilizational studies lies in his being both an astute critic and a harbinger of harsh developments to come, as between power centers and their inner and outer peripheries. Such unfolding developments must be taken into account by scholars who wish to understand the swift dynamics of a modern history increasingly inexplicable in positivist or Marxist terms. The non-Marxist Pitirim A. Sorokin pioneered in such accountings, which have great relevance to the transformations taking place everywhere, especially those in Eastern Europe and in Sorokin's native land. Sorokin's prophetic vision comprehends mostly adverse circumstances impinging upon, undoing, or transforming sociocultural value systems. American contemporaries engage more with propitious circumstances that reinforce, confirm, and enrich standing value systems. In short, Sorokin's rough dialectic provides a context within which more novel changes emerge from cultural dialectics between strands of traditions.

My use of the term "dialectic" (with its explicit or implicit qualifier "rough") sidesteps a range of philosophical or even sociological uses of the term from Hegel and Marx on. The notion of the "radial contrariety" is original, perhaps idiosyncratic. Such "rough dialectic" in the largest sense (not unlike Toynbee's "challenge-and-response"), and in the more limited cultural interchange sense, as well as all the other contrarieties, are at the service of a mediating intervention between Sorokin and his critics, one shaped by American philosophical interests. Such mediation, to put it mildly, is Neo-Sorokinian, and is motivated by the belief that Sorokin has much to leave for American and cross-cultural thought.

As for the City, Cosmopolis, and Modernity, the allusion is to centralized wealth and power as amplified by science and technology, and as suspect in the eyes of hinterlanders and outlanders. Sorokin's somewhat sniffy use of "sensate" emerges here as the quality of the City's bait for suckers; empiricist epistemologists really shouldn't have their feelings hurt. One last thought is this: progressive dialectics provide cultural change analogous to William James's "once-born" religious experience; rough dialectics, along with the occasioning vast disruptions, may yield transformations of a "twice-born" type.

Fifteen

POSTSCRIPT ON THE RADIAL CONTRARIETY

It became obvious to me that more had to be said about the radial contrariety than appeared in my Centennial presentation. Because of its simplest expressions, my colleagues, Ford and Richard, took it as an overly simple distinction, whereas it is all-pervading in American culture, political and popular, and largely accounts for Sorokin's wide-spread impact. The complementarity between rough and progressive dialectics also draws deeply upon this polarity.

The philosopher Immanuel Kant, seeing that natural science was actual, asked how it was possible. In answering, his method was a Transcendental Deduction. If we ask, somewhat in the manner of Wilhelm Dilthey, how empathetic understanding (*Verstehen*) is possible for the human sciences, the answer will be an inductive one that is virtually inevitable. The question could be posed again in this way: How is psychic mobility (among values) possible? I shall suggest an answer, which, incidentally, might furnish some useful equipment for facing the issue of relativism.

Briefly, great imaginative leaps—including those required for cross-civilizational study—however variable in their actual success, are made possible by practice jumps. And practice jumps are forced upon us by all sorts of contrarieties or polarities into which life and culture thrust us. The radial contrariety, only one of these, is by far the most colorful coordinate as it encourages greater freedom than do the others, since hinterlanders and outlanders are usually under less direct central control than urban underdogs.

The metaphor "radius" applies to the line reaching out from centers of power, however broadly construed, toward their inner and outer peripheries containing hinterlanders and outlanders. Along with the vertical polarities of social or economic classes, the radial expressions, explicit or implicit, are encountered in life, in art whether high or low, in inherited religions largely encapsulated from distant regional origins, and in political traditions and present-day practices.

The markings of psychic mobility are explicitly or implicitly polar. Some cultural expressions are so pronouncedly one thing that what they *are* not is obvious: such as a regionalist who is unsophisticated. Regional and urban poles need not always be at war. As warlike instances, we may cite Mao's militant countryside surrounding the cities before 1949 and his later Cultural Revolution, or American colonies in revolution against their home power. But neither are they typically and happily harmonized as in the film *Meet Me in St. Louis,* where local boosterism and family triumph over New York's temptations. More usually, there is some tension, awkwardness, satire, at least one-upmanship; the regional sage twitting the City on corruption or the worldly scholar deploring provincial backwardness. (The *Washington Post* ran a hayseed cartoon when the Carters came to the White House, and ignored Rosalyn's mental health program.)

On the simplest level of popular culture, dualities are marked between the country mouse and the city mouse, Mortimer Snerd and Charlie McCarthy, Snuffy Smith and Barney Google, the Clampetts and the Drysdales, the Douglases and Mr. Haney in "Green Acres," implicitly in "Hee Haw," as with the satiric use of "Grand Old Op'ry," with the current vogues of country as well as Western music, Western films (sometimes featuring a city-slicker-type villain), and so on. What is striking even in such rudimentary forms are the contrasting regional and urban values, however simplified they are for easy recognition. More subtle and dynamic interplays between those poles and those of the vertical contrarieties of social and economic class appear in serious literary and dramatic works, throwing strong reflective light on social and political questions across space, time, and class difference. Leo Tolstoy, Mark Twain, and other deeply rooted regional writers work in interesting ways with value contrasts. Picaresque stories, showing fictive movements among regions and class backgrounds, examples of the *Bildungsroman* (which includes *War and Peace*), comedies of manners, as in Fielding, Sheridan, Trollope, and Austen, all display the radial contrariety even though the vertical social contrariety may be the dominating one. (For the British this is certainly more the case than for Americans.)

Popular art, fiction, drama, and films can be said to employ conventional place markers for power centers and peripheries. The complexities of real, or supposedly real, internalizations of the radial vector are richer than any static duality. With lively internalizations of the vector a highly creative ambivalence can arise.

Consider three examples for such ambivalence. José Ortega y

Gasset combined a cosmopolitan goal with regional affirmations. He saw "Europeanization" as needed to overcome Spain's isolation, while at the same time he affirmed the artistic and traditional values of *hispanidad*. Pitirim A. Sorokin fused Westernizing and Slavophil ideals, merging the Comtean and Tolstoyan influences. Where such masterful scholars came down in their judgments and preferences is a subtle matter indeed. Tolstoy himself had been greatly influenced by the Enlightenment, this shaping his heretodox views, but his preponderant message was Slavophil.

Creative ambivalence also may be imputed to any number of persons whose roots are regional and whose aspirations and achievements are urban. Many Americans look back nostalgically at their origins, even while looking ahead to careers in some power center. The radial contrariety plus the temporal vector does generate strong nostalgia, as do Stephen Foster's songs, including that traditional Kentucky Derby opener, "My Old Kentucky Home," and Thomas Wolfe's *Look Homeward Angel* and *You Can't Go Home Again*. The American point of view typically synthesizes an overlay of urban values upon a regional core. Sometimes urbanists forget, or repress, that core.

The radial contrariety is quite various in its expressions. What about romance? Romance in terms of the radial contrariety can be found in Chaucerian *fabliaux*; in farmer's daughter and traveling salesman stories; in Marian the librarian and Professor Harold Hill of *The Music Man*; in *Tillie's Punctured Romance* where Marie Dressler, an implausible farm girl, is jilted by a city slicker played by Chaplin; in Little Em'ly of Yarmouth and James Steerforth (a class differentiation is dominant here: "I won't come back until he makes me a lady"); Natasha Rostov and the Frenchified officer from St. Petersburg; Rachel Wardle of Dingley Dell and the strolling player Jingle; etc., etc. A really fine example of the radial, social, and economic contrarieties intermixed for a short British TV series was the romantic social comedy *To the Manor Born*. The heroine, Audrey, was country gentry of higher social status, the hero who rented her country estate was urban, and deplorably *nouveau riche*. Fortunately for the plot, he was provided with a matchmaking mother.

The radial contrariety in some forms goes way back. One summer out in a Kentucky mountain region, an old gentleman approached me, King James version in hand, to advance his Bible-based view that more tornadoes hit the cities than the countryside because of urban wickedness. Now, that may be defective meteorology and deplorable moral theology, but it's a fine example of the radial contrariety in its most adversarial mode. It rings truer than does the theologian Harvey Cox's *Secular City* (1965), which flatters the urban consciousness.

What sorts of biblicist traces are there which might have fed such regionalist one-up-manship? Jewish, Christian, and even Muslim communities began on the outer fringes of ancient high civilizations, Egypt, Babylon, Rome, and Constantinople. Lacking their wealth and power, hinterland prophets consoled themselves with the purity of their own monotheisms and their eventual providential triumphs.

Egypt, with its "flesh pots," was put in its place; Babylon had its fateful handwriting on the wall. Jesus himself was a hinterlander, from the Jerusalem point of view; "Can any good thing come out of Nazareth?" His cleansing of the Temple can be seen as exemplifying the radial contrariety, a purist's impatience with the needs of currency exchange and commerce. Other contrarieties of the vertical sort, those of economic class (the rich and poor, markedly in the Lucan gospel) and of status (righteous followers of Torah and sinners), were strategically woven together with the radial contrariety by Jesus in prophetic efforts to bring the "people of the land" back into an ideally solidary Jewish community. He heightened the internalized moral demands, about which Joseph Klausner said that he exaggerated Judaism, and made available Divine forgiveness for all who fall short, erstwhile respectable citizens and "people of the land" alike. (This strategy was later shifted by Paul to suit the needs of Gentiles.) My point is that the radial vector does not monopolize culture but is, at least, a quite necessary alloy. Mohammed rejected the learned Trinitarian teachings of the Orthodox empire as tritheism; had he accepted them, it would have been political as well as religious deference given to that empire. His goal, and that of his successors, was conquest and purification, reaching its high mark in 1453, but by no means its termination, as today's news of jihad shows us. Overall, biblicist thematics tend to show virtue out yonder and vice in the city. For his part, Martin Luther took Renaissance papal power as a re-awakening of the "Whore of Babylon," so the donation of Constantine turned out to be double-edged, as had Augustine's caustic comments about the City of Man.

The radial contrariety can enter literary and historical legends, in terms of the movement of a regional hero toward a center of power and its subsequent conquest. The southern boy Elvis Presley and the Corsican "Man of Destiny" Napoleon hold considerable popular fascination for that reason; "Local boy makes it in the Big Time." There is more color here than in any merely vertical conquest, as in Horatio Alger's newsboy story, *Rags to Riches*. *Les Invalides* and Graceland both remain impressive shrines for the enthusiasts. There is even heroic questing in an invented myth; Tolkien's Frodo Baggins sets out from the Shire (clearly based on regional England) against the evil Mordor (palpably suggested by urban pollution and the "dark Satanic mills.")

The homeward quest can also have its own heroic standing: Dorothy struggling to return to Kansas; Ulysses seeking Ithaca; and on a humbler, less stressful, level, the happy "going-home" songs that are counterparts to sad nostalgia ballads. George Gershwin's "Swanee" is a joyful transformation of Foster's "The Old Folks at Home." It finally goes, "The folks up North will see me no more, when I get to the Swanee shore!" And an ethically judgmental element can enter, as in Gene Autry's "Back in the saddle again, back where a friend is a friend!", presumably according to purer regional *Gemeinschaft* (or community) as opposed to impersonal urban *Gesellschaft.* Kropotkin's "mutual aid" and Russian *sobornost* are influences for Pitirim Sorokin's own ideationally grounded altruism, as opposed to the contractual ethos of the sensate (and over-urbanized) era.

What about politics? Such adversarial clues as we have just considered betoken sharpened polarizations at the level of politics and political thought. Major dualities become generated both here and abroad. In ancient China, along with temporal (or generational) and class vectors influencing the mandarin teachings, the radial contrariety had brought regional Taoism up against Confucianism of the power center. Anti-bureaucratic and anarchistic suggestions were thus leveled against the central power and its intelligentsia. Sorokin picked up on some of those insights in his own critiques of late sensate governmental power. And very contemporary Chinese continue their regional attacks upon urban corruption, sometimes as one-up-manship in the current leadership struggle.

Two political dualities, one from the United States and the other from Russia, are of special significance to us since Sorokin's incomprehension of Americans, and American incomprehension of Sorokin, follow largely from their difference. Over here, we have the radially based "Populism–Progressivism" contrast, the first regional and the second urban and modernist. Over there, from the early years of the twentieth century, there was the radially based "Anarchism–Authoritarianism" polarity.

Sorokin, as a rural sociologist, reasonably enough pointed out the deep incompatibilities in LaFollette's Farmer-Labor Alliance. More broadly, regional populists and urban progressives would seem to have little basis for cooperation. That there was any New Deal at all seems to have been, like the bumblebee, an aeronautical impossibility. Clearly, Sorokin was drawing on his awareness of Social Revolutionary and Social Democrat cleavages, as based on rural/urban divergence.

The question is this: how is it that two expressions of the radial polarity, American "Populism–Progressivism" and Russian "Anarchism–Authoritarianism," work so differently, the first so congenially receptive to synthesizing harmony, as in Wisconsin politics and the New Deal, and the second so irreconcilable? The difference, sadly enough, seemed to have put any effective alliance between Pitirim A. Sorokin, the Russian-born ex-Social Revolutionary and sociologist, and urban American liberals out of the question during Sorokin's lifetime.

The Russian autocracy had arisen as a military defense against marauding invaders from the West, South, and East. Its authoritarian structure, while successful enough against intrusions from without, generated reformist and populist opposition from within. Its hinterlanders, sometimes conquered peoples themselves, could not be satisfied. Americans, however, especially after the Late Unpleasantness drastically settled the agrarian slavery question, were generally homogenous and free from external threat. Beyond that, their regional hinterlands had bargaining powers in the Congress, mandated by the composition of the Senate. Regional statesmen could strike deals with other regional statesmen, and thereby enforce tolerable arrangements with urban power centers, whether executive or economic. Henry Clay and Alben Barkley of Kentucky, Daniel Webster of New Hampshire, Lyndon Johnson of Texas, Walter George and Richard Russell of Georgia, Russell Long of Louisiana, and other weighty examples of regional dealmaking statesmanship come to mind. Governmental and business power centers had to come to terms with such men and usually wisely did so. An example of a brief regional–urban clash came in 1944 when Alben Barkley resigned as Majority Leader (after a rude veto message from Roosevelt) and was unanimously re-elected to tumultuous applause. Roosevelt tactfully backed down with the famous "Dear Alben" letter.

Much more can be said, from the American point of view, about political aspects of the radial contrariety. Political campaigns seek to roust out hinterland voters in vast numbers, either for a candidate seen as attractive to them, or against some city-slicker-type aligned with robber barons given to wicked trusts, or with bankers who oppose silver coinage, or with corrupting inside-the-Beltway bureaucrats or lobbyists. The railsplitter, born-in-a-log-cabin image, Honest Abe or Old Hickory, campaigns by front porch or whistle stop or bus–all of this can be deployed in a markedly down–home way. After the 1992 national election, Gore Vidal, himself a distant cousin of the new vice president, wrote a shrewd article about Clinton and Gore as Huck Finn and Tom Sawyer. Beyond this, I observed that in the 1994 congressional election at least two Virginia representatives, Rick Boucher and L.F. Payne, managed to resist a Republican sweep, in part, by ads to the effect, "He's one of us." Despite shrill cries by their opponents "He's not one of us, he's one of them!" they both managed to make it. Here, regional self-identification played a major role, local interests against big city temptations.

This seeps out into the popular culture: think of the animated cartoon rooster character Foghorn Leghorn. He is a direct takeoff of Kenny Delmar's Senator Claghorn in Fred Allen's "Allen's Alley." What is the point? The preservation of a regional accent is a decided political asset for Americans, whereas an accent is a social liability over in England. In John Mortimer's *Paradise Postponed*, Leslie Tittmus, the aspiring Conservative politician, goes to great lengths—while laughing at himself—to acquire a "posh" accent. That counts as evidence that the vertical social contrariety is more basic for Britons than the radial one; the reverse being true for Americans. Again, the phrase "He's one of us" has a class-based connotation more often than not for the English, while (at least at election times) it's regionally-based for Americans.

Recognition signals, however simple they may be, play their part in social and political alignments. Loretta Lynn actively campaigned for George Bush against Michael Dukakis, as Grand Old Op'ry stars had earlier done for Richard Nixon. The serious component here was *The New Republican Majority* thesis set forth by Kevin Philips. The Democrats having made themselves vulnerable on matters like affirmative action, Republican hopes, stalled briefly by Watergate, are increasingly vested in regions, Southern or Western or Midwestern. Their awkwardly big-city, Wall Street affiliations can be counted on to be downplayed. Political advertising, ironically supplied by big-city firms, can be relied upon to flatter the crudest regionalist sensibilities, whichever party is running. Ross Perot, that cornpone billionaire, clearly influenced everyone's thinking and copycat versions are bound to arise.

Lastly, oscillating attention between polar values dynamizes the contrarieties, radial or vertical, providing the counterpart to atomic, or perhaps molecular, energy for the great wheeling constellations in the sociocultural domain; that is, Worldviews or guiding visions. Perspectivism can be kept respectable, given an operative *Verstehen* in Diltheyan or neo-Diltheyan, neo-Sorokinian terms. It operates at quite different levels of sophistication, as the preceding discussion suggests, but always as conveying and organizing values, all in defiance of nihilism.

Sixteen

SOROKIN AND THE WORKINGS OF CULTURATIVE SYMBOLICS

This chapter was revised for the 1994 Comparative Civilizations meeting in Dublin, modifying its first form when read for the Society of Asian and Comparative Philosophy.

One key piece of the puzzle is its examination of recent ethnic and religious conflicts–further evidence for Sorokin's prognosis of late sensate breakdown. Currently, it is pseudo-ideational, rather than ideological, fanaticism in the post-Cold-War world that endangers our planet.

Another important element that looks toward the unifying conclusion is the discussion of selected West European philosophers who focus on history and cultural change. They illumine the way cultural elements, recipients, and creators are attended to, and this is very much akin to Sorokin's "superorganic" dimension. Their emphases contrast with Dewey's and Randall's more naturalist orientations, and their philosophic acuity contrasts with Sorokin's more rough-and-ready approach to the history of ideas.

Alternating religious and secular emphases have taken place in history. This thought is well expressed, along with unfavorable and favorable attitudes, respectively, by Oswald Spengler and Arnold Toynbee. With much supportive detail and subtlety, Pitirim A. Sorokin, for his part, characterizes the rhythms of, or oscillations between, "ideational" (religious) culture and the "sensate" (or "this-worldly") type.

"Culturative symbolics" is an apt characterization for both "ideational" and "idealistic" sociological types. (The idealistic serves as an intermediate between the ideational and sensate). Philosophy of culture is currently of much relevance, given today's convulsive interactions among diverse civilizational traditions. What is meant by culturative symbolics? It can be given this rough accounting: expressions that somehow commend, change, sustain, or organize ways of life and thought. Such expressions persuasively transmit norms and values, their fullest and most imposing types appearing as philosophical or religious systems. Some philosophical systems persuasively commend themselves *as* culturative, others commend a dryer objective goal–cognitive symbolics.

One assumption made here is that cognitive symbolics, which manifestly includes common sense knowledge as well as science, is rather less helpful for comparative philosophy than is the more humanistic and wide ranging culturative symbolics. By and large, empiricisms, positivisms, and scientific realisms see themselves as having built upon very specific achievings and receivings between humans and nature, rather more than upon shapings and transmissions of historical culture. Philosophical types which most strongly express the culturative function are as follows: Platonisms, rationalisms, idealisms, and many phenomenological approaches. These primarily attend to the meaningful roles and normative patterns socially transferred between persons. Admittedly, science is cultural and (at least latently) carries its own norms, its special commended ways of inquiry. But the larger supportive enframements and normative highlightings found in projective systems tend to be down-played by recent philosophers; skeptical withdrawals, even from the modest epistemological projections called foundationalisms, have been pursued vigorously by logical empiricists and by contemporary analysts. These attacks denigrate the status of speculative systems, whether culturatively ideal or cognitively naturalistic.

The boundary between culturative and cognitive symbolics can be drawn only in a rough approximation. Joseph Campbell had said that myth has its mystical, sociological, and cosmological functions. The first two of these, one relating humanity to some ultimate reality and the next providing and commending social norms, surely seem to suggest culturative symbolics, the third more clearly bespeaks cognitive symbolics. Again, a philosophical system persuasively conveys, commends, or transfers principles, thus it has its formative, as well as transformative, and informative aspects; that formative aspect matches the sociological, the transformative the mystical, and the informative the cosmological (or cognitive). Sorokin's "ideational" and "idealistic" supersystems are fittingly illumined by culturative symbolics, while his sensate culture, with its empiricist orientation, favors cognitive symbolics and often an instrumentalist approach. All significant human learning seems to be either strikingly culturative or else notably cognitive, or a mix of the two.

Twentieth-century thinkers who developed culturative symbolics can now be mentioned. Wilhelm Dilthey's treatment of experience, expression, and understanding, along with his triadic analysis of philosophical types, had provided helpful structural elements for culturative symbolics. Neo-Kantian Ernst Cassirer held a broader view of symbolism than did most of his contemporaries. His "philosophy of symbolic forms" amounted to a rich theory of culture, embracing science, art, history, religion, as well as political and civic "myths." His historicizings and expansions of Kant notably updated the Marburg legacy. His student Suzanne K. Langer carried on and refined his theory of art, especially in the realm of *poesis*, through which many patterns of life can be commended or otherwise weighed. Later, her original evolutionary philosophy of mind correlated with cultural trends in pre-history and history.

Karl Jaspers made his significant contributions in three ways: firstly, in his elucidating modes of the Comprehensive; secondly, in his discussion of the creative Axial Age; and thirdly, in his examination of "great philosophers." (The influence of his friend Heinrich Zimmer, the distinguished scholar of Indian thought, is detectable in Jaspers's openness to Eastern philosophy.)

Reminiscent of many of the preceding contributions was the work of Pitirim A. Sorokin. Sorokin put markedly Neo-Platonic elements into discussions of ideational and idealistic values, often given their shape under Tolstoyan influences. But, as a sociologist, Sorokin was keenly aware of conditions reinforcing or disrupting the "internalization of norms." Sorokin can be said to Platonize or Neo-Platonize the three stages of Auguste Comte (the theological, the metaphysical, and the positive) by giving a highly favorable valorization to the first two, by celebrating them as "ideational" and "idealistic." He refrained from making the three phases strictly cyclical, but he does affirm more flexible "rhythms" or "oscillations" in their succession. Consistently with his personal involvement in peasant life and religious art, and his deep distrust of Bolshevik regimes, not to mention his later reaction against America's "roaring twenties," he finds the "sensate age" to be in deep crisis. "Cynical sensate" and "pseudo-ideational" phenomena reinforced this contention, which was given full development in *Social and Cultural Dynamics* and ramified in later works.

Confirmations of Sorokin's theses regarding the decline of sensate culture may be seen in the collapse of satellite and Soviet Communism, the accentuation of "fundamentalist" tendencies in the Middle East, recent murderous religiously based wars in Bosnia and

Northern Ireland, India, Sri Lanka, etc., in the supplanting of a secularist Iranian Shah by an Ayatollah, in the Trade Center bombing and the fanatical killing of tourists in Egypt, not to mention the rise of a "Christian Right" in the United States. Unfortunately, his Tolstoyan ideas led to an overly-idyllic concept of ideational possibilities. But Sorokin *did* allow that most results of "polarization" under crisis were negative ones. That seems the case today, with false prophets stridently in the majority.

A good way to place culturative symbolics would be to look back at Dilthey's not precisely Hegelian use of "objective spirit." When he used that phrase, Dilthey emphasized the concrete expressions and material embodiments of culture; appropriately enough, so did Sorokin while discussing the material, natural "vehicles" of meaning. On the other hand, Hegelians look more to the Ideality than to its actual expression. Consider Benedetto Croce on art, and Suzanne K. Langer on "semblance," an aspect lifted apart from its natural artistic embodiment and thereby from the causal context.

The scope of subject matter for culturative symbolics appears most fully in Hegelian "Absolute Spirit"; that is, in terms of Art, Religion, and Philosophy. Such complexes of meaning, among their many functions, manifestly commend and transmit ways of life. Then, with his stress upon Ideality rather than upon the actualities within which the complexes are embodied, Hegel, not unlike Plato, points us toward a key to unlock the puzzle of cultural complexes.

The best key is the metaphor of "projection." There were some early peoples who projected their deities into the celestial domain, distinct in its distance and purity from messy terrestrial actualities. Plato was clear, however, that his exalted "Sun of the Intelligible World" was not the same as the one in our sky. (Take the term to an obvious current use; "projection" literally throws various light images on the dingy silver screens that are purchased by theater owners and cleaned by janitors. But the upper-case "Silver Screen" is a domain highly regarded by enthusiasts and populated by extraordinary fictive characters. Here Ideality is other than actuality.) On one hand, philosophic projections may be divergent, that is turned away from actuality; but as mergent, they may be thrown as overlays into worldly actuality (Taoism, Stoicism, Spinozism); or they may be partly mergent and partly divergent (Cartesianism). This reading seeks compatibility with Dilthey's "worldview theory," which in fact takes Cartesianism as a bridging type.

Divergent, let us say transcendent, projections draw our attention through their Otherness. Generalizing across types of transcendent projections into Ideality, high-level cultural complexes, especially when elaborately value-laden, must be scrutinized and analyzed quite apart from their concrete expressive embodiments, their material causes and effects. Their virtual elements must be construed both in relation to one another *and* to the cultural incipient/recipient (subject). (For religious traditions the aforesaid "self-involvement" may be mediated, as through ancestors or forerunners.) The "aesthetic point of view" involves the self minimally in a contemplative mode; religion deeply involves selves both personally and communally. By contrast, philosophical systems target the self simply as knower.

Putting to one side that simple analysis, which ignores mixtures among the types, we can still find clear marks of projectival "Otherness." Often there are imputed matrices for those projections markedly contrasting with those of the everyday. Even such technical terms as Teilhard's "noosphere" and Sorokin's "superorganic" carry a qualitative apartness from the ordinary. More noticeably, from the arts come phrases like "aesthetic distance," "once-upon-a-time," "Never-never land," "Utopia," "Otherwhere," "the Twilight Zone"; from religions, the "Supernatural," Heavens (not as equivalent to outer space), Times before Time (primordial myths as respecting, for example, the "Dream Time"), Last Days or Eschatons, the "Sacred Void" as in Buddhism, and the timeless Platonic Realm of Forms. All of the preceding terms variously betoken transcendence. Analogous clues to projective immanence, though more subtle, could also be given their own inventory.

Sorokin's "ideational" and "idealistic" cultural supersystems have a congenial fit with projective transcendence. Sorokin is more sympathetic to ideational and idealistic forms than to the sensate. His sympathy patently appears in his affirming of "integralism" as the best philosophy, wherein the highest values of all supersystems would be synthesized. Neo-Thomism is one position whose adherents may naturally be drawn to integralism. On the occasion of the American Sociological Association's 1963 write-in presidential vote for Sorokin, many Catholic sociologists turned out in his favor.

Sorokin's prediction of an ideational turn was grounded in a "principle of limits." Going too far in one direction led to acute distortions and crises. Still more profoundly interesting was his "law of polarization," whereby calamities bring many negative along with only a few positive results. Religious and moral creativity, "altruization," occasionally does manage to appear under adverse conditions. Overall, Sorokin's prognosis has worked out remarkably well. Much that has happened supports it. Concretely, politico-economic changes have opened the door for ideational movements, though too often of unfortunate sorts. Secular empires have surprisingly retreated, leaving room for communities to re-identify themselves along religiously differentiated lines. The ideological framework sustaining the Cold War has either collapsed entirely, as in Eastern Europe and the former USSR, or it has been so weakened that ideological factors have been often subsumed *under* theocratic principles. (In the United States, regnant capitalism has shown its weaknesses while the Republican Party has been virtually taken over in certain locales by the "Christian Right," fueled by high-powered televangelism.)

Whereas earlier self-images were more based on secular, or "sensate," principles, this has been drastically undermined, opening options for various "Old-Time Religions." Belief that our children will be better off economically has virtually disappeared; older (and imported) faiths have roughly pushed to the fore. That many of these are "pseudo-ideational" is cold comfort in this market for militant other-worldliness.

The obvious danger of the ideational turn comes with the fierce conflicts among religious communities and sects, the sort of thing that led Locke to denounce "enthusiasm." Dogmatic exclusivisms preclude negotiated settlements on the basis of higher shared values or even rational self-interest. That makes the case for loosening up doctrinal absolutes and for moving steadily toward the acceptance of viable religious pluralisms. The positive side of ideational culture, according to Sorokin, lies in its creative mysticism and "altruization," not in its battle cries for Holy Wars based on assumptions of Holy Monopolies.

One should then look for positive ideational content as the alternative to anti-scientific and destructive forms. Socially benign and creative mystical elements appeared in Leo Tolstoy's thought, in that of Mohandas Gandhi, and that of Martin Luther King, Jr. Other such exemplary leaders and thinkers include Martin Buber, Albert Schweitzer, and Good Pope John. Astute analyses of creative mysticism were made by Henri Bergson, William James, Max Otto, and others, and by Pitirim A. Sorokin when he and fellow researchers were examining altruism. Sorokin's "L. N. Tolstoy as a Philosopher" shows the primary Tolstoyan influence on his interpretation of ideational and idealistic cultural supersystems. His overly idyllic reading of ideational phases and movements no doubt forgivably comes from selective attention upon its very best expressions.

Reflective critique of culturative symbolics, applied to religious but also philosophical systems, could be therapeutic in countering dogmatic versions of some One True Faith, of an absolute Reality-Picture, which can easily generate persecutions of heretics and unending wars against the infidels. The metaphor of projection must be taken properly; no pictorial image is really projected, but rather an orientation strategy, one that is hopefully well founded. Any such system is offered as the best bet on values made by some series of sages and prophets. Religious differences are not at all to be seen just on a cognitively perspectival model, as with the Indian fable of the blind men and the elephant. Functional analogues, but not identities, are to be looked for among such vast orientative strategies, and if the inquirer is lucky, sometimes a felicitous complementarity may be found as an interfaith bridge. The projective transcendence of great religious visions forbids taking any of them literally, that is, subsuming such culturative visions *under* the pattern of cognitive symbolics.

How helpful are the metaphors "worldview" and "perspective?" Discriminations are necessary: where philosophies are concerned, non-Platonic realisms, naturalisms, and empiricisms rightly claim to be cognitive at a manifest level and thus fit the metaphors, as do many or most ideologies. Thus, so far, Ninian Smart's use of the term "worldview" would seem persuasive. But any culturative projections such as the great religions, and philosophic approaches which are predominantly idealistic, Platonic, or rationalist, do not seem cognitive at the manifest level. To the extent that they relate to knowledge, it is more at the level of "deep structure." The Pauline condition is that "Now we see as in a glass darkly." It is not that those culturative projections are non-cognitive, but that they cannot be taken as cognitive symbolics purely and simply. Clashing truth claims are not to be fought out in any simple-minded, or literal way. While intolerance may be more comforting, its destructive effects are becoming too manifest.

When comparing key themes in cultural systems, one can fall into the temptation of identifying them. Sometimes, this misidentification turns out to be helpful in limited ways, but its basis is always a functional analogue between distant cultural workings. Culturative symbolics must then judiciously sort out and weigh such analogues *and* disanalogues alike. Items in one tradition sometimes are within shouting distance of cultural items in another, and while not strictly capable of assimilation, they may be not unlike the "latching-on" aspects of those philosophies which fuse dialectically into what is mistakenly seen as static "perennial philosophy." But cross culturally speaking, the most favorable expectation one can have is of some measure of cultural distance, but without any insurmountable barrier to understanding. Culturative symbolics assists in reaching across the still noticeable distance.

Seventeen

CONCLUSION: THE ROUGH AND THE SMOOTH

Progressive dialectics, reflecting how science, technology, and social innovations steadily ratchet the human condition upwards, seems smooth by contrast to the rough, crisis-punctuated, fluctuations of Sorokin's accounting. How do we take the rough with the smooth? Western Europeans and Americans incline to progressivism; so how is Sorokin to be made available to them? How are rough and progressive dialectics to be reconciled? On one side stands Sorokin, on the other, among others, are Auguste Comte, Talcott Parsons, and John Herman Randall, Jr. Large issues of social and philosophical change have been scanned up to this point. Now the time has come to force some of the pieces of the puzzle together.

Three steps are indicated, each taken with some mounting difficulty. The easiest is to look at issues of plain common ground; the next is to find interpretive mediations between apparent differences, ultimately capable of reconciliation; while the third is to see how unmediatiable differences complement each other on different time scales and in quite different perspectives. The radial contrariety, in its most ample deployment, serves as an essential tool in that final search for complementarity.

As for common ground between Sorokin and progressive thinkers, much of that was staked out by Sorokin himself in his "Similarities and Dissimilarities," written about Parson's compared to his own theories. This was earlier mentioned for its appearance in *Fads and Foibles* (1956b) and in *Sociological Theories of Today.* That shared ground is found in two very different books, Parsons's *The Social System* (1951) and Sorokin's *Society, Culture, and Personality* (1947). Briefly, their views jointly spell out key conceptual interactions for the discipline of sociology not yet available in Comte's positivist work, even in more recent naturalist approaches. Values are central for them, in several significant dimensions.

Where Sorokin deals with the "internalization of norms" and with manifest values, Parsons engages in parallel discussions, but concentrates on professional standards and ethical norms, offering an American sublimation of Max Weber, as with his Protestant ethic. A basic commonality for our purposes throughout this book had to do with the social emulation of manifest normative patterns for choice (the Good) or for role-fulfilment (the Right). On what was referred to as the "midscale" level of commendable ways of life, Sorokin and Parsons make their impressive joint appearances in elucidating such matters.

In part, Sorokin overlaps with Comte; of course not with his unilinear theory overall, but with the progressive trend in the earlier phases of unfolding sociocultural supersystems. Sorokin concedes high creativity to the first four centuries of our sensate era, indeed, to powerful mixed creative and decadent tendencies lasting to the end of the nineteenth century. Other more conservative theorists prefer to deplore everything since William of Ockham, assuredly since the French Revolution. Sorokin regarded liberalizations more favorably, though these social goods are rendered problematic by the gradual breakdown of contractual standards. This helps explain why his "conservative Christian anarchism" finds limited favor with self-proclaimed cultural conservatives. Once, seeing the interest of *Modern Age* in Leo Strauss and Eric Vogelin, I proposed submitting a Sorokin comparison. The current editor was surprised and even indignant. Evidently, Sorokin was not sufficiently anti-liberal; a strict follower of Le Maistre may have fared better. In any case, Sorokin engaged in co-affirming ideational, idealistic, and sensate values at their very best. This complex integralism renders sentimental advocates of the Ancient Regime somewhat puzzled.

Another overlapping affinity can be discovered in Tolstoy, and by inference in Sorokin: that with American liberal Protestantism. Unitarianism gave rise to Transcendentalism; both were matrices for our own emerging Cambridge pragmatism. Tolstoy's religious and philosophic speculations, although tinged with a distinct monastic asceticism, otherwise comport well with the anti-Orthodox and highly personal styles of Emerson and of Emerson's younger friend, William James. Sorokin's final location in Cambridge must have awakened remarkably interesting historical echoes, despite any disagreements with pragmatists of a later generation.

Interpretive bridges should now be thrown up and mediation pursued. Apparent differences are capable of resolution, given sufficient help and effort. The main characters will be Sorokin and John Herman Randall, Jr., with a number of Western European philosophers called upon to give corroborative evidence. The central themes will be creative dialectic, and overlapping with this, the quite problematic nature of "perennial philosophy." How is so-called perennial philosophy, strictly speaking, mis-called, and what was the temptation to do so? Once we follow that line, Sorokin and Randall wind up far less at odds than first impressions suggest. Both emphasized cultural change, and cultural change keeps philosophy from being "always the same."

A step toward isolating the nature of "creative dialectics," and of so-called "perennial philosophy," is to concentrate upon culturative symbolics, insofar as doing so projects enframements for ways of life and thought. In subtle but significant ways those issues intrigue both Sorokin and Randall.

A cloud of witnesses mediates between Sorokin and Randall. Wilhelm Dilthey, Benedetto Croce, Ernst Cassirer, Karl Jaspers, and José Ortega y Gasset share relevant virtues, one of which is appreciation of Kant, also another, sympathies with Sorokin's and Randall's cultural themes. As these magisterial European philosophers focus upon history and culture, this protects them from static epistemological and dry metaphysical gridlocks. In this, they resemble Randall, but they have a greater sense of civilization's vulnerability, and in that respect are closer to Sorokin. As Western Europeans, they fall between optimistic Americans and the more somber Russian. Sorokin's emphasis accords well with their sensitivities to the humane studies. What they say about culture amplifies Sorokin's views, and even qualifies some of his seeming simplifications with more specifically philosophical and European evidence.

What about the projective aspect of culturative symbolics, where pure cultural elements get the predominant emphasis at the expense of natural contexts, materials, and contingencies? Always with us, as Sorokin points out, are biophysical agents of cultural action and "material vehicles" of meaning. Yet apart from these, the "superorganic" dimension, like the Platonic realm of Forms and the ideality of Hegelian Absolute Spirit, in art, philosophy, and religion, focuses our attention upon, and orientates us to, our cultural context. We find ourselves in Nature, but, just as importantly, in Culture. Cognitive symbolics emphasizes the first, the most congenial for naturalists; culturative symbolics stresses the second, the sort more sympathetically received by Platonists and idealists. Randall and Sorokin acknowledge both, but allocate their importances somewhat differently.

Consider how Auguste Comte denigrates the theological and metaphysical stages of thought, how Dewey argues against both supernaturalism and transcendentalism in his *Quest for Certainty*

(1929), but how Sorokin seeks to rehabilitate ideational and idealistic sociocultural supersystems. Sorokin departs from Comte more decisively than Randall does from Dewey, but Randall had been greatly influenced by his own father, a theological modernist, also by F. J. Woodbridge, a historian of philosophy subtly sympathetic to Plato, and by A. C. McGiffert, a great liberal Protestant historian of Christian thought. By comparison with Randall, Dewey demonstrated a rather foreshortened and tendentious grasp of intellectual history.

Randall takes a striking position regarding Plato's Theory of Forms and Hellenistic religious philosophies in general. As a Deweyan, he does not fall under the spell of classical or medieval essentialism, but characterizes Aristotle in functionalist terms. He highly praises Plato not as a metaphysician, but as a poet and great "Dramatist of the Life of Reason" (Randall 1970). He takes an affirmative attitude toward religion in its promotion and unifying of human values (Randall 1958, p. 122). Religion is like art, but not subordinated to it, and like Plato's work, at its best it is Wisdom. That does not leave Randall too far distant from Sorokin, who does still discover ideational and idealistic "truth." Randall's non-cognitivism stops short of that but, in terms of axiology, the two scholars think along quite similar lines (Randall 1958, pp. 140ff.).

Randall and Sorokin are not doing just the same thing, but they have much more in common than first strikes the eye. Randall's notion of the dialectic between science and institutional values is broader than that he once suggested in his *Making of the Modern Mind*. According to his account, Platonic science enters into various Hellenistic religious syntheses, as did Platonistic science into Christian theology (1970a, p. 140). We may not read the modern kinds of wholesale science-inspired, transforming change back into Hellenistic and medieval times, although the rediscovery of Aristotle did stimulate a creative Renaissance science to which Randall turned his attention.

But Randall's progressive dialectic, like that of his teacher Dewey, does not lead into any dogmatically secure once-and-for-all "perennial philosophy." Since Sorokin allows that his own thought is a "mere variation of perennial strains in philosophy," is he in disagreement on this point with Randall? (Allen 1963, p. 373). The answer is surprisingly negative. Why not? Sorokin's rough dialectic simply cannot issue into any fixed essentialist doctrine, his integralist sympathies are too widely distributed among cultures, and his oscillation theory too pronouncedly subject to variation.

The key is this: Randall and Sorokin are both deeply anti-authoritarian, resistant then to any rational authoritarianism–for example, classical essentialisms or Thomism, even in more moderate expressions. Their versions of dialectic, one progressive and the other rough, each entail open-ended creativity as traditions merge, whether from the promise of science and new organizations, or from the rough shakings of historical adversity. Creative dialectic manifestly issues then from the rough and the progressive varieties.

Of West European mediators between Randall's and Sorokin's positions, Karl Jaspers seems the most striking. His Kant-influenced "principles of philosophic faith" connect him to the liberal Protestant background of Randall, while his psychocultural reflections match well with Sorokin's sociocultural interests. Jaspers's *Umgreifende* (or Comprehensive) should be identified with William James's "more" and with Sorokin's Superconscious as the source of creative intuitions. The creative dialectic which is common to Sorokin and Randall may also, in its most significant expressions, be appropriately read in terms of Jaspers's work on the Axial Age and the "great philosophers."

Randall's lectures on Plato and Plotinus, which I heard at Columbia, and his two books on Platonic and Hellenistic thought (1970a, 1970b) constitute a strong affirmation of the prime importance of Wisdom and the merging of rich traditions that yield enhanced Wisdom. His emphasis on religion as unifying values (1958, p. 102) matches up well with Sorokin's Integralism. Both Randall and Sorokin, despite all their apparent differences, are forward-looking as to social and concomitant cultural change, provided that such developments worthily follow the precedents of past creative fusions, not just in letter but in spirit.

We can sum up affinities among Sorokin, Jaspers, and Randall, underlining key points. Sorokin's treatment of the Superconscious suggests both continuity with the self (immanence) and Transcendence. Sorokin was subject to the Tolstoyan influence; Tolstoy's immanental "Kingdom of God is within you" theme became pivotal for Sorokin's ideational culture.

Jaspers's Comprehensive, on the face of it, is mainly immanental, although Transcendence appears as one of its modes. Randall expresses some sympathy toward Platonic and Platonistic "Wisdom," even though he stops short of characterizing "myth" in terms of truth or falsity. Nonetheless, Randall's taking religions as helpfully unifying human values not only calls to mind the Platonic One as the source of values, but also Sorokin's Integralism, that takes the Superconscious as the origin of cultural creation. Sorokin's "meanings-values-norms" include cognitions; that marks his difference from Randall's mild non-cognitivism.

The sociocultural, when regarded in and of itself, still implies biophysical agents and material vehicles of meaning, so the superorganic, or spiritual, domain cannot literally be "other-worldly." So affinities are grounded between Sorokin, the naturalist Randall, and the phenomenologist Jaspers, and this circumstance validates Integralism. Furthermore, the Superconscious correlates with socio-cultural awareness, just as the unconscious does with the bioconscious. Sorokin must not be misread as a dualistic medievalist, nor should William James, whose use of "Superconscious" appears in *Varieties*, as does his reference to a "more" continuous with consciousness. (Religious modernists, coming out of American Protestantism, such as the two Randalls, could not escape the Jamesian influence.)

To expound on the circle of affinities, to forge another link in the chain, let me point out that Sorokin takes creativity as the test for intuitions from the Superconscious. Creativity involves novelty and positive value: creative dialectic is a fortunate fusion of traditions under lucky circumstances. Randall does not talk of the Superconscious, but he does recount creative instances of philosophical and religious fusions. That is dialectical circumstantial evidence for grouping Randall with Sorokin. What help is talk about "perennial philosophy" in light of the need to steer between dogmatism and nihilism? There is no "once-and-for-all" true cultural system, but perennially there is guiding philosophy that differs in its forms. Among cultural enframements, similar structures and functions give "latching-on" points for dialectical convergences into creative novelty.

Creativity precludes mere repetition, but dialectical continuity prevails among converging traditions. Such reinforcement among systems allows us to speak of "perennial philosophy." Ideational and idealistic systems do much the same sort of thing, in which all systemic instances differ, though carrying analogous functions. Sorokin's self-ascription of "mere variation of perennial strains of philosophy" to his Integralism shows that cultural change is no mere whim.

Having sought out bridges between Sorokin and worthwhile expressions of modernity, by way of palpable and not so palpable common ground, we turn to the question of complementarity. How does Sorokin's work balance off against, and compensate for, insightful forms of urban progressivism? Here the most available instance, already developed in earlier chapters, is that of Talcott Parsons, whose rational liberalism, like the sophisticated empirical liberalism of Randall, stands at the urban pole of the radial contrariety. Sorokin was the prophetic outsider; his diagnoses and prognoses reflected the all-too-well-remembered vulnerability of hinterlanders and outlanders. In convulsive times, the peripheries pay a much heavier price than do the regnant power centers. And professional spokespersons for the City, backed by the power and wealth which implement their burgeoning expertise in technology and management, are less likely to foresee the City's decline. Indeed, in and through crises, mid-level urban experts are more likely than hinterlanders to land on their feet, having notable transferable skills, as did Leonardo and Werner von Braun, not to mention mandarins of China shifting to new dynastic loyalties.

Perspectivally speaking, Sorokin's macrosociology (or historical sociology) takes a long-range look at history. Talcott Parsons's structural-functionalism takes an intermediate-range look, one that presumes the continuity of urban control, or rather exemplary leadership, for hinterlands and "developing" outlands. This allows the urban professionals, and those who anticipate joining their meritocracy, a sustainable confidence. (This throws light on why the Harvard Department of Social Relations refrained from requiring Sorokin's course as a pre-requisite. Parsons was a progressive Confucius for modernity; no rough-hewn "Taoist" need apply.)

We have mentioned ideas shared between Parsons and Sorokin, where conceptual enrichment advances the field beyond Comtean positivism to awareness of the distinctive sociocultural dimension and of the "internalization of norms." Sorokin departed early on from any localized, or practical, microsociology and joined the company of more wide-ranging and free-wheeling "social philosophers." This group had, as Sorokin indicated in a book title, responded to an "age of crisis."

Where is the complementarity, really, between Sorokin and Parsons? One cannot simply scissors-and-paste together their two tales of the City and other matters, hoping for coherence. Their different purposes lead to differences in perspective, scale, and scope for their magisterial theories. For starters, they write for different audiences, set at poles apart on the radial contrariety. But more is at stake than their separate constituencies. Rational scholarly needs lie behind their work, not just satisfying the whims of partisan groups. Furthermore, the account has to be fully generalizable to make explanatory sense for other instances of rough and progressive dialectic than theirs.

Parsons and Sorokin, as had been earlier suggested, each offer serious answers to sets of serious problems. For example, progressive theories (including that of Parsons) address the needs of advanced and advancing urban backers to rationalize and incorporate economic development with social management. The demands of modernity for theoretically-grounded assurance and advice have become ever more pressing over the past two hundred and fifty years. Those with the responsibility, or even the hope, of exercising power call upon progressive dialecticians from the Encyclopedists on. In his time, Parsons left much of lasting value for the urban leaders through his structural-functionalism.

Magnetizing effects of worldwide modernizing speed-ups upon progressive dialectics, including Parsons's theories, are obvious. Less obvious to modern Americans are the historic forces which strongly call forth rough dialectics. First of all, most of the globe is hinterland or outland, with respect to already "developed" or "Westernized" power centers. Secondly, "every action has an opposite and equal reaction" must be applied to historic changes dynamizing everything, among which are the surviving Great Traditions more and more abrasively reacting and jostling one another. "Social philosophies of an age of crisis" rightly respond to forces now awakened on the peripheries of modernity; Spengler, Toynbee, and Sorokin, all practitioners of rough dialectics, looked beyond Eurocentrism. Also broad in their views, comparative studies of all sorts embrace the range of new and old, examining incidental cultural side effects of convulsions, though sometimes in rudimentary or piece–meal fashion. Rough dialectics addresses and hopefully prescribe for, the wounds inflicted by modernity's cutting-edge. In particular, Sorokin's philosophy of value both describes and prescribes for modernity's messes. In the long run, its accommodation to American thought has to be sought in the broadest context.

Modernity has its discontents, within itself as intensified ambition, and against itself as strong peripheral reactions. So it is that, aggravated by unremitting change, the radial contrariety yields a double stimulus, from the power centers for progressive dialectics, and from their peripheries for the rougher sort. Glittering promises of, and disruptions from, modernity call forth two modes of thinking. This duality energizes social sciences (Parsons and Sorokin), but principally, popular and public philosophies (Sorokin, Spengler,

Toynbee, *et al.*). Sorokin's and other rough dialectical approaches engage general audiences sympathetic to hinterland or outland values, more than regular academics, whose hopes conform to urban power.

Americans can best balance the values of smooth and rough dialectics through hinterlander perspectives softened by discriminating urban sympathies. To fill this bill, liberal Protestants and later modernists can mediate Sorokin and Parsons, also Sorokin and Randall. Why? They hark back to hinterland sects, whose hinterland forerunners reacted to pagan urbanism. But unlike Fundamentalist cousins, these adherents became subtly "citified," and so able to appreciate both poles of the radial contrariety. Equally important is America's "*E pluribus unum*" legacy, where regionalists were given a place at the urbanist table. That good fortune insures a tolerance for progressive dialectics, while attacks on passive and cynical sensate values, and the media which purvey them, are not suppressed. Sorokin's and Parsons's two tales of the City are available as moral guidance to liberal Protestants and regionalists. So are Sorokin's and Randall's only slightly polar accounts of cultural and intellectual change.

Still, there is good news and bad news. The Cold War being over, ideological dogmatisms which once prevented Sorokin's historical sociology from getting any kind of a fair hearing are evaporating. What is the bad news? Grievance-settling interest groups have rushed in to fill that vacuum with propaganda based on ancient ethnic rivalries. But whatever that present recrudescent ideational clamor, America's greater good fortune, at least as compared with Russia's, at the best of it, should permit her a centrist alignment on the radial contrariety, along with some salutary smoothing down of Sorokin's roughest pronouncements. The previous ideological polarity, based mainly upon the urban-centered vertical contrariety, had little to offer in resolving City-versus-regional differences, and practically nothing at all to say regarding the ancient peripherally-based Great Traditions, the antique energies of which are now being released with equivocal force in places of civilizational overlap. American liberals, whose experience of the radial contrariety has been less rough than Sorokin's, should gird themselves to face such challenges. Sorokin's life-work can be attuned to assist them.

Post-Darwinian natural history has shown that in life there are no absolutely fixed truths. Likewise, in the lurchings about and innovative mutations of human history, there are no final dogmas to be had. Sorokin and Randall, anti-authoritarian as they rightly are, both recognize this. From their different angles, backgrounds, and disciplines, both steer well clear of the dogmatist's rocks and the nihilist's whirlpool. The falsity of dogmatism does not entrail the truth of nihilism. No Perennial Philosophy has the last word, though perennially there has to be philosophy as the unifying vision of values, cognitive and otherwise. Rough and progressive dialectics both show how these unifications, precious but precarious, are called forth. Sorokin even speaks of the Superconscious as involved in the calling forth of their best examples. But oscillations of cultural systems continue; likewise from the angle of liberal empiricism, fallibilism is the watchword.

Parsons had an exalted vision of what the science of social action could do; Sorokin's hopes for historical sociology or macrosociology also ran high, but in different directions. For all the overlaps in their thinking, and the parallels between integralism and rational liberalism, Sorokin stands closer to Randall on the larger questions, any appearances to the contrary notwithstanding, than to Parsons. Americans, to best attune their ears to Sorokin, should explore empiricist and rationalist liberalisms in their full historical contexts, and try to work free of Eurocentrism, all in the light of the larger questions that have no simple or final answers. Any system, however worthy, is an interim report, and a future ingredient for creative dialectics.

WORKS CITED

Alexander, Jeffrey. (1983) *Theoretical Logic in Sociology.* Vol. 4. Berkeley: University of California Press.

Allen, Philip ed. (1963) *Pitirim A. Sorokin in Review.* Durham: Duke University Press.

Anderle, Othmar, ed. (1964) *The Problems of Civilizations: Proceedings of the International Society for the Comparative Study of Civilization at Salzburg.* The Hague: Mouton.

Ayer, A. J. (1948) *Language, Truth, and Logic.* London: Gollancz.

Bergson, Henri. (1911) *Creative Evolution.* Translated by Arthur Mitchell. New York: Holt and Co.

——— (1955) *Introduction to Metaphysics: The Perception of Changeability.* Translated T. E. Hulme. New York: Liberal Arts Press.

——— *(1971) Time and the Freedom of the Will: Introduction to Metaphysics.* Translated by F. L. Pogson. London: G. Allen and Unwin.

Broad, C. D. (1953) "Critical and Speculative Philosophy," Pp. 75-100 *in Contemporary British Philosophy,* 1st and 2nd series. Edited by H. Muirhead. London: G. Allen and Unwin.

Burtt, E. A. (1965) *In Search of Philosophical Understanding.* New York: New American Library.

Caponigri, Robert A. (1955) *History and Liberty.* London: Routledge and Paul.

Christian, William A. (1964) *Meaning and Truth in Religion.* Princeton: Princeton University Press.

Copleston, Frederick. (1982) *Religion and the One.* New York: Crossroad Publishing Co.

Cowell, F. R. (1972) *Values in Human Society.* Boston: Porter Sargent.

Cox, Harvey. (1965) *The Secular City.* New York: MacMillan.

Croce, Benedetto. (1940) *A History of Europe in the Nineteenth Century.* New York: G. Allen and Unwin.

——— (1955) *History as the Story of Liberty.* New York: G. Allen and Unwin.

——— (1962) *My Philosophy.* New York: Collier.

——— (1963) *A History of Italy:* 1871-1915. New York: Clarendon Press.

——— (1970) *A History of the Kingdom of Naples.* Chicago: University of Chicago Press.

Eliade, Mircea. (1978) *A History of Religious Ideas,* Vol. 1. Chicago: University of Chicago Press.

Ermath, Michael. (1978) *Wilhelm Dilthey: The Critique of Historical Reason.* Chicago: University of Chicago Press.

Ewing, A. C. (1953) *Ethics.* New York: Free Press.

Ford, Joseph, Michel Richard, and Palmer Talbutt, eds. (1955) *Sorokin and Civilization: A Centennial Assessment.* New Brunswick, N.J.: Transaction Press.

Friedrichs, Robert. (1970) *A Sociology of Sociology.* New York: Free Press.

Hallen, G., and R. Prajad, eds. (1972) *Sorokin and Sociology.* New Delhi: Moti Katra.

Halliday, E. M. (1958) *The Ignorant Armies.* London: Weindenfeld and Nelson.

James, William. (1908) *The Varieties of Religious Experience.* New York: Longmans, Green, and Co.

——— (1954) *Pragmatism.* New York: Literary Press.

Jaspers, Karl. (1954) *The Way to Wisdom.* New Haven: Yale University Press.

Jaworski, Gary. (1993) "Pitirim A. Sorokin: Sociological Anarchism." *History of the Human Sciences,* 6:3 (March), pp. 61-77.

Johnston, Barry V. (1995) *Pitirim A. Sorokin: An Intellectual Biography.* Lawrence: University Press of Kansas.

Jonas, Hans. (1963) *The Gnostic Religion,* 2nd ed. Boston: Beacon Press.

Katz, Steven, ed. (1978) *Mysticism and Philosophical Analysis.* New York: Random House.

Kennedy, Paul. (1987) *The Rise and Fall of the Great Powers.* New York: Random House.

Körner, Stephen. (1984) *Metaphysics: Its Structure and Function.* Cambridge: Cambridge University Press.

Lazerowitz, Morris. (1955) *The Structure of Metaphysics.* London: Routledge.

Lewis, H.D., ed. (1963) *Clarity Is Not Enough.* New York: Humanities Press.

MacIntyre, Alasdair. (1986) *Whose Justice? Which Rationality?* Notre Dame: University of Notre Dame Press.

Maquet, Jacques J. (1951) *The Sociology of Knowledge.* Boston: Greenwood Press.

Matilal, Bimal. (1971) *Epistemology, Logic, and Grammar in Indian Philosophical Analysis.* The Hague: Mouton Press.

McNeill, William H. (1963) *The Rise of the West.* Chicago: University of Chicago Press.

Megill, Allan. (1985) *Prophets of Extremity.* Berkeley: University of California Press.

Melko, Matthew and Leighton Scott. (1987) *The Boundaries of Civilization in Space and Time.* Lanham, Md.: University Press of America.

Montague, A. (1956) *Toynbee and History.* Boston: Porter Sargent.

Nisbet, Robert A. (1970) *Social Change and History.* New York: Oxford University Press.

Organ, Troy Wilson. (1976) "Polarity, a Neglected Insight in Indian Philosophy," *Philosophy East and West,* 26:1 (January), pp. 33-39.

Parks, Robert E. (1938) "Review of Pitirim A. Sorokin, *Social and Cultural Dynamics.*" *The American Sociological Review,* 43:6 (December), pp. 824-32.

Passmore, John. (1967) "Philosophy." *The Encyclopedia of Philosophy*, Vol. 6. Edited by Paul Edwards. New York: Macmillan. Pp. 216-29

Perry, Ralph Barton. (1912) *Present Philosophical Tendencies.* New York: Greenwood Press.

Petrazhitsky, Leon. (1908) *Introduction to the Study of Law and Morality.* St. Petersburg.

Potter, Karl. (1992) *Presuppositions of India's Philosophies.* Westport, Conn.: Greenwood Press.

Radhakrishnan, Sarvepalli. (1978) *Eastern Religious and Western Thought.* London: Oxford University Press.

Randall, John Herman, and John Herman Randall, Jr. (1929) *Religion and the Modern World.* New York: Frederick A. Stokes Co.

Randall, John Herman, Jr. (1927) *The Making of the Modern Mind.* New York: Houghton Miflin.

——— (1937) "Review of Pitirim A. Sorokin, *Social and Cultural Dynamics.*" *The American Sociological Review,* 42 (December), pp. 921-24.

——— (1958) The *Role of Knowledge in Western Religion.* Boston: Beacon Press.

——— (1963) *How Philosophy Uses Its Past.* New York: Columbia University Press.

——— (1970a) *Hellenistic Ways of Deliverance and the Making of the Christian Synthesis.* New York: Columbia University Press.

——— (1970b) *Plato: Dramatist of the Life of Reason.* New York: Columbia University Press.

Rickert, H. (1910) "On the Concept of Philosophy." *Logos*, 1.

Scharfstein, Ben-Ami, *et al.* (1978) *Philosophy East/Philosophy West.* New York: Oxford University Press.

Shils, Edward. (1980) "Some Academics: Mainly at Chicago." *The American Scholar* 50:2 (March), pp. 179-96.

Simmel, Georg. (1892) *Die Probleme der Geschichtsphilosophie.* Leipzig: Duncker und Humboldt.

——— (1911) *Hauptprobleme der Philosophie Leipzig.* Leipzig: Duncker und Humboldt.

Skinner, B. F. (1972) *Beyond Freedom and Dignity.* New York: Knopf.

Smart, Ninian. (1973) *The Phenomenon of Religion.* London: Herder and Herder.

Smith, John E. (1968) *Experience and God.* New York: Oxford University Press.

Sorokin, Pitirim A. (1914) *L. N. Tolstoy as a Philosopher* [in Russian]. Moscow: Russian Comradeship Press. (Translated by Lawrence T. Nichols, 1997. See this volume.)

——— (1927) *The Sociology of Revolution.* New York: H. Fertig.

——— (1937-41) *Social and Cultural Dynamics,* 4 vols. Boston: Bedminster Press.

——— (1941) *The Crisis of Our Age.* New York: E. P. Dutton Press.

——— (1944) *Russia and the United States.* New York: E. P. Dutton Press.

——— (1948) *The Reconstruction of Humanity.* Boston: Beacon Press.

——— (1950a) *Modern Historical and Social Philosophies.* New York: Dover Press.

——— (1950b) *Social Philosophies of an Age of Crisis.* Boston: Beacon Press.

——— (1954) *The Ways and Power of Love.* Boston: Beacon Press.

——— (1956a) "Integralism Is My Faith." In *This Is My Faith.* Edited by Whit Burnett. New York: Harper.

——— (1956b) *Fads and Foibles in Modern Sociology.* Chicago: Regnery.

——— (1957) *Social and Cultural Dynamics.* One volume ed. Boston: Porter Sargent.

——— (1957b) *The American Sex Revoluation.* Boston: Porter Sargent.

——— (1963) *A Long Journey.* New Haven: Yale University Press.

——— (1964) *The Basic Trends of Our Times.* Boston: Beacon Press.

——— (1965) "Sociology of Yesterday, Today, and Tomorrow." *American Sociological Review,* 30:6 (December) pp. 833-43.

——— (1966) *Sociological Theories of Today.* New York: Harper and Row.

——— (1975) *Hunger as a Factor in Human Affairs.* Translated by Elena Sorokin. Gainesville: University Press of Florida.

Sorokin, Pitirim A., and Walter Lunden. (1959) *Power and Morality.* Boston: Porter Sargent.

Sorokin, Pitirim A., and Carle Zimmerman. (1927) *The Principles of Rural-Urban Sociology.* New York: H. Holt and Co.

Sorokin, Pitirim A., Carle Zimmerman, and C. J. Galpin. (1930-32) *A Systematic Source-Book in Rural Sociology,* 3 vols. Minneapolis: University of Minnesota Press.

Strakhovsky, Leonid I. (1944) *Intervention at Archangel.* New York: H. Fertig.

Talbutt, Palmer. (1980) "Sorokin vs. American Thought." *Sociologia Internationalis,* 18:1-2 (October), pp. 5-20.

——— (1981) "Theology and the Gentile Tradition." *Encounter,* 41:3 (July), pp. 237-61.

——— (1986) *Reanimation in Philosophy.* Lanham, Md.: University Press of America.

——— (1988) "Biblical and Gentile Tensions." *Encounter,* 45:1 (July), pp.61-65.

Tibbs, A. E. (1943) "Book Reviews of *Social and Cultural Dynamics*: A Study in *Wissensociologie.*" *Social Forces,* 21:2 (May), pp. 473-80.

Tolstoy, L. N.(1881 [1887]) *The Way of Life.* St. Petersburg: Mediator Press.

——— (1905 [1961]) *The Kingdom of God Is Within You.* Translated by Leo Wienêr. New York: Farrar, Straus, and Cudahy.

——— (1914) *What Is Art?* New York: Liberal Arts Press,

Toynbee, Arnold. (1961) *Reconsiderations.* Vol. 12 of *Study of History.* New York: Oxford University Press.

——— (1974) *Toynbee on Toynbee.* New York: Oxford University Press.

Troyat, Henri. (1965 [1967]) *Tolstoy.* Translated by Nancy Amphoux. New York: Doubleday Harmony Books.

Urmson, J. O. (1967) "J. L. Austin." In *The Linguistic Turn.* Edited by Richard Rorty. Chicago: University of Chicago Press. Pp. 232-38.

von Laue, Theodore H. (1969) *The Global City.* New York: Lippincott.

Zimmer, Heinrich. (1969) *Philosophies of India.* Princeton, N. J.: Princeton University Press.

ABOUT THE AUTHOR AND CONTRIBUTORS

Lawrence T. Nichols, whose translation of the Sorokin essay on Tolstoy and whose Centennial presentation on Tolstoy's influence upon Sorokin add so much to this volume, received his Ph.D. from Boston College in 1985, with emphases on criminology and social change. He has been teaching at West Virginia University. A member of Phi Beta Kappa, he has taught Russian at St. Louis University. He is the co-author of *Corporate Policy; Values and Social Responsibility,* (1985), and *Beyond the Courtroom: Programs in Community Justice and Conflict Resolution* (1981).

Nichols has published widely regarding social problems, criminology and deviance, business ethics, sociological theory, and the history and sociology of social science. In 1992 he was awarded a National Endowment for the Humanities fellowship to conduct a seminar on social problems. An active reviewer, he was especially helpful to the International Society for the Comparative Study of Civilizations, whose *Festschrift* honoring Sorokin *(Sorokin and Civilization: A Centennial Assessment,* 1995) greatly depended upon his devoted service. He continues groundbreaking research on Sorokin, publishing illuminating treatments of E. A. Ross and Pitirim A. Sorokin, their agreements and their differences.

Pitirim A. Sorokin, the author of "L.N. Tolstoy as a Philosopher," is given biographical treatments in the first, second, and fifth chapters of this volume.

Palmer Talbutt, Jr., the principal author of this book, born in 1927 of central Kentucky stock, went through public school in northern Kentucky, effectively in a suburb of greater Cincinnati. He served in the Marines for thirteen months, having been drafted before V.J. Day. Through a scholarship, he went to Harvard, majoring in English, with seven philosophy electives. Having taken modern and Russian history under the distinguished scholar Michael Karpovich, he found Pitirim A. Sorokin's sociology course a fine capstone to his college education. Subsequently, he took his master's degree in philosophy at Columbia, emphasizing history of thought and philosophy of culture, enabling him to study Sorokin's work at greater length. Further academic work at Garrett was followed by a doctorate from Duke. He taught at Pembroke State College, North Carolina, and part-time at Duke University. He joined the Department of Philosophy and Religion at Virginia Tech in 1959. (Only a few elective courses were then offered.) While in Blacksburg, he met and married Lou Ella Culler; their son, Scott Cummins, was born in 1973.

Talbutt participated in the bringing about of an expanded curriculum and an undergraduate major in philosophy, teaching a wide variety of courses over the years, chairing library and personnel committees, specializing in such fields as ethics, philosophy of history, American philosophy, aesthetics, philosophy of religion, phenomenology and existentialism, among others. In 1979 he began an active and continuing role in the International Society for the Comparative Study of Civilizations, and in 1987 proposed the Centennial sessions in Sorokin's honor. In 1995 *Sorokin and Civilization*, co-edited by Ford, Richard, and Talbutt, appeared. His other activities included papers delivered to the Virginia Philosophical Association, the Southern Society for Philosophy and Psychology, the Society of Christian Philosophers, the American Association of Philosophy Teachers, and the Society for Asian and Comparative Philosophy. Thirty-three papers were read, nine articles and four reviews were published, along with one book, *Reanimation in Philosophy* (1986), and the co-edited book on Sorokin previously mentioned. Upon retirement in 1991, Talbutt became Associate Professor Emeritus of Philosophy.

INDEX

VIBS

Titles Published

1. Noel Balzer, *The Human Being as a Logical Thinker.*

2. Archie J. Bahm, *Axiology: The Science of Values.*

3. H. P. P. (Hennie) Lötter, *Justice for an Unjust Society.*

4. H. G. Callaway, *Context for Meaning and Analysis: A Critical Study in the Philosophy of Language.*

5. Benjamin S. Llamzon, *A Humane Case for Moral Intuition.*

6. James R. Watson, *Between Auschwitz and Tradition: Postmodern Reflections on the Task of Thinking.* A volume in **Holocaust and Genocide Studies.**

7. Robert S. Hartman, *Freedom to Live: The Robert Hartman Story,* edited by Arthur R. Ellis. A volume in **Hartman Institute Axiology Studies.**

8. Archie J. Bahm, *Ethics: The Science of Oughtness.*

9. George David Miller, *An Idiosyncratic Ethics; Or, the Lauramachean Ethics.*

10. Joseph P. DeMarco, *A Coherence Theory in Ethics.*

11. Frank G. Forrest, *Valuemetrics: The Science of Personal and Professional Ethics.* A volume in **Hartman Institute Axiology Studies.**

12. William Gerber, *The Meaning of Life: Insights of the World's Great Thinkers.*

13. Richard T. Hull, Editor, *A Quarter Century of Value Inquiry: Presidential Addresses of the American Society for Value Inquiry.* A volume in **Histories and Addresses of Philosophical Societies.**

14. William Gerber, *Nuggets of Wisdom from Great Jewish Thinkers: From Biblical Times to the Present.*

15. Sidney Axinn, *The Logic of Hope: Extensions of Kant's View of Religion.*

16. Messay Kebede, *Meaning and Development.*

17. Amihud Gilead, *The Platonic Odyssey: A Philosophical-Literary Inquiry into the* Phaedo.

18. Necip Fikri Alican, *Mill's Principle of Utility: A Defense of John Stuart Mill's Notorious Proof.* A volume in **Universal Justice.**

19. Michael H. Mitias, Editor, *Philosophy and Architecture.*

20. Roger T. Simonds, *Rational Individualism: The Perennial Philosophy of Legal Interpretation.* A volume in **Natural Law Studies.**

21. William Pencak, *The Conflict of Law and Justice in the Icelandic Sagas.*

22. Samuel M. Natale and Brian M. Rothschild, Editors, *Values, Work, Education: The Meanings of Work.*

23. N. Georgopoulos and Michael Heim, Editors, *Being Human in the Ultimate: Studies in the Thought of John M. Anderson.*

24. Robert Wesson and Patricia A. Williams, Editors, *Evolution and Human Values.*

25. Wim J. van der Steen, *Facts, Values, and Methodology: A New Approach to Ethics.*

26. Avi Sagi and Daniel Statman, *Religion and Morality.*

27. Albert William Levi, *The High Road of Humanity: The Seven Ethical Ages of Western Man,* edited by Donald Phillip Verene and Molly Black Verene.

28. Samuel M. Natale and Brian M. Rothschild, Editors, *Work Values: Education, Organization, and Religious Concerns.*

29. Laurence F. Bove and Laura Duhan Kaplan, Editors, *From the Eye of the Storm: Regional Conflicts and the Philosophy of Peace.* A volume in **Philosophy of Peace.**

30. Robin Attfield, *Value, Obligation, and Meta-Ethics.*

31. William Gerber, *The Deepest Questions You Can Ask About God: As Answered by the World's Great Thinkers.*

32. Daniel Statman, *Moral Dilemmas.*

33. Rem B. Edwards, Editor, *Formal Axiology and Its Critics.* A volume in **Hartman Institute Axiology Studies.**

34. George David Miller and Conrad P. Pritscher, *On Education and Values: In Praise of Pariahs and Nomads.* A volume in **Philosophy of Education.**

35. Paul S. Penner, *Altruistic Behavior: An Inquiry into Motivation.*

36. Corbin Fowler, *Morality for Moderns.*

37. Giambattista Vico, *The Art of Rhetoric* (*Institutiones Oratoriae,* 1711-1741), from the definitive Latin text and notes, Italian commentary and introduction by Giuliano Crifò, translated and edited by Giorgio A. Pinton and Arthur W. Shippee. A volume in **Values in Italian Philosophy.**

38. W. H. Werkmeister, *Martin Heidegger on the Way,* edited by Richard T. Hull. A volume in **Werkmeister Studies.**

39. Phillip Stambovsky, *Myth and the Limits of Reason.*

40. Samantha Brennan, Tracy Isaacs, and Michael Milde, Editors, *A Question of Values: New Canadian Perspectives in Ethics and Political Philosophy.*

41. Peter A. Redpath, *Cartesian Nightmare: An Introduction to Transcendental Sophistry.* A volume in **Studies in the History of Western Philosophy.**

42. Clark Butler, *History as the Story of Freedom: Philosophy in Intercultural Context,* with Responses by sixteen scholars.

43. Dennis Rohatyn, *Philosophy History Sophistry.*

44. Leon Shaskolsky Sheleff, *Social Cohesion and Legal Coercion: A Critique of Weber, Durkheim, and Marx.* Afterword by Virginia Black.

45. Alan Soble, Editor, *Sex, Love, and Friendship: Studies of the Society for the Philosophy of Sex and Love, 1977-1992.* A volume in **Histories and Addresses of Philosophical Societies.**

46. Peter A. Redpath, *Wisdom's Odyssey: From Philosophy to Transcendental Sophistry.* A volume in **Studies in the History of Western Philosophy.**

47. Albert A. Anderson, *Universal Justice: A Dialectical Approach.* A volume in **Universal Justice.**

48. Pio Colonnello, *The Philosophy of José Gaos.* Translated from Italian by Peter Cocozzella. Edited by Myra Moss. Introduction by Giovanni Gullace. A volume in **Values in Italian Philosophy.**

49. Laura Duhan Kaplan and Laurence F. Bove, Editors, *Philosophical Perspectives on Power and Domination: Theories and Practices.* A volume in **Philosophy of Peace.**

50. Gregory F. Mellema, *Collective Responsibility.*

51. Josef Seifert, *What Is Life? The Originality, Irreducibility, and Value of Life.* A volume in **Central-European Value Studies.**

52. William Gerber, *Anatomy of What We Value Most.*

53. Armando Molina, *Our Ways: Values and Character,* edited by Rem B. Edwards. A volume in **Hartman Institute Axiology Studies.**

54. Kathleen J. Wininger, *Nietzsche's Reclamation of Philosophy.* A volume in **Central-European Value Studies.**

55. Thomas Magnell, Editor, *Explorations of Value.*

56. HPP (Hennie) Lötter, *Injustice, Violence, and Peace: The Case of South Africa.* A volume in **Philosophy of Peace.**

57. Lennart Nordenfelt, *Talking About Health: A Philosophical Dialogue.* A volume in **Nordic Value Studies.**

58. Jon Mills and Janusz A. Polanowski, *The Ontology of Prejudice.* A volume in **Philosophy and Psychology.**

59. Leena Vilkka, *The Intrinsic Value of Nature*.

60. Palmer Talbutt, Jr., *Rough Dialectics: Sorokin's Philosophy of Value*, with Contributions by Lawrence T. Nichols and Pitirim A. Sorokin.